A Balanced Christian Life

WATCHMAN NEE

Translated from the Chinese

Christian Fellowship Publishers, Inc.
New York

ISBN 0-935008-53-5

Available from the Publishers at:

11515 Allecingie Parkway
Richmond, Virginia 23235

PRINTED IN U.S.A.

TRANSLATOR'S PREFACE

"Ephraim is a cake not turned" (Hosea 7.8). This is a figurative way of saying "not balanced." The cake is burned on the one side, uncooked on the other; on one side it is overdone, on the other, totally undone. The cake is unfit to be eaten and is thus destined to be cast out.

Our God is most balanced. He is love and He is light. Our Lord Jesus is full of grace and full of truth. The Holy Spirit is the Spirit of wisdom as well as of revelation. In creation, God "hath measured the waters in the hollow of his hand, and meted out heaven with a span, and comprehended the dust of the earth in a measure, and the hills in a balance" (Is. 40.12). Concerning redemption, it is said that "mercy and truth are met together, righteousness and peace have kissed each other. Truth springeth out of the earth; and righteousness hath looked down from heaven" (Ps. 85.10,11). The new creation, therefore, must be well balanced.

In this present volume, Watchman Nee attempts to show from God's word the perfect equilibrium of divine truth. Human nature, however, is prone to emphasize one side to the exclusion of the other side of truth. This has caused much confusion and many problems among God's people. It is essential that we know the balance of truth and hold on to both sides so that our Christian life may be well-rounded as God has ordained.

The contents of the book opens with a treatment of the balance between the gate and the way; continues with a presentation of the balance between the objective and the subjective; includes a discussion on the work inward and the work outward in the Christian life, as well as on the rest given and the rest found as promised by Christ; contemplates the other side of prayer frequently neglected, namely, to watch; and concentrates on the other less emphasized aspect of the trespass-offering, that of restoration. The book then provides a commentary on the contrast between the truly meek and the spiritually poor, and finally concludes with a consideration of the equilibrium that is so necessary between the believer's faith and the believer's walk.

May all who read this volume be brought into a balanced Christian life.

CONTENTS

This is a collection of ten messages given by the author at one time or another throughout the years of his fruitful ministry. Because of the relatedness of their content in terms of balance in the Christian life, they are now being translated and published together in English as a single volume.

Scripture quotations are from the
American Standard Version of the Bible
(1901), unless otherwise indicated.

1 The Gate and the Way

> Enter ye in by the narrow gate: for wide is the gate, and broad is the way, that leadeth to destruction, and many are they that enter in thereby. For narrow is the gate, and straitened the way, that leadeth unto life, and few are they that find it. (Matt. 7.13,14)

Our purpose today is not to explain the above passage but to show instead the course of the Christian life. For these two verses touch upon two great principles: (1) entering the gate, and (2) walking in the way. To emphasize either one of them to the exclusion of the other will result in an extreme. God puts before the Christian a gate and a way or a way and a gate in order to keep him in balance.

What is the meaning of entering the gate? To enter the gate is to pass through a crisis. Just as a gateway has a gate which stands against your progress, so passing through that gate means getting through to something which you have never experienced before. No matter how thick is the gate, it does not take five minutes to pass through it. As soon as a person passes through, he is immediately in a different environment. There is a vast difference between what is the scene before he passes through the door and what it is afterwards. Five minutes ago he was in one particular world; but now he is in a different world. Formerly the person was outside the gate, currently he is within it. For example, outside Jessfield Park* can be seen dust and cars. But once a person enters the park gate, he instantaneously senses he is in a totally different realm. Hence, spiritually speaking, entering the gate signifies that within a very brief period of time there comes a tremendous difference. In that very short duration, a Christian has passed through a crisis and his spiritual condition takes instantly a different turn.

A Christian has not only to go through a crisis, he has a way to walk along as well. The way is long and requires much time to walk along it. Does it take much time to enter the gate? Obviously, it can be passed through in swift order. Which, then, requires the longer time—to enter the gate or to walk in the way? Naturally, walking in the way requires more time. It becomes highly unbalanced if one enters the gate without taking any step along the way thereafter. After the Christian enters the gate, he must walk forward step by step. Walking in the way means to proceed gradually one step after another. To enter the gate needs only one step, but to walk in the way can-

*A public park in a suburb of Shanghai.—*Translator*

not be done in just one step. Upon entering the gate, therefore, the Christian immediately senses a distinctive change. He goes forward, perhaps a hundred steps more, and then he may have to pass through another gate. Perhaps a thousand steps farther, and still another crisis awaits him. A Christian must therefore be prepared to walk the way whenever he decides to enter a gate. Hence to enter the gate means to go through a crisis, while to walk in the way means to make progress.

Today there is much controversy among Christians on this matter. Some emphasize crisis, whereas others emphasize progress. Some consider entering the gate to be the supreme experience, while others assume they may proceed without any need of entering the gate. Both are unbalanced positions. We ought to know that on the one hand we need to go through a crisis and on the other hand we need to proceed on the way. Entering the gate and walking in the way are two important principles in the Bible. They must be equally stressed.

According to God's word, in our spiritual course, entering the gate precedes walking in the way. First the crisis, then the progress. Yet this is the very opposite to most any earthly journey, for the latter usually calls for walking before entering. For instance, you must first walk along Hardoon Road before you enter the gate of Wen Teh Lane and arrive at the meeting place for worship. In the spiritual journey, however, this is not the case. It can instead be likened to a journey towards a palace or a royal mausoleum that has a tremendous wall around it.

You need to enter the gate first, then advance along a lengthy pathway before you reach your destination. Since the Bible always puts the gate and the way together, we may see them at work in both "faith" and "obedience"—two key principles of the Christian life.

Faith

Faith is a principle of our Christian walk. Faith is governed by two rules that are represented by a gate and a way. All who are familiar with spiritual experience know that faith is composed of "believe" and "trust." There is a difference between the *act* of faith and the *attitude* of faith. To believe once and for all is what we call passing through a crisis, but to trust continuously afterwards is what we call making progress. Exercising a single-minded act of faith is entering the gate, but maintaining an attitude of faith thereafter is walking in the way. In order for a Christian to truly believe in God in a particular matter, he must with singleness of heart first exercise an act of faith by which he truly believes in God before he can ever walk the way of faith. In entering the gate of faith he crosses a threshold of doubt, and thus with single-heartedness he receives from God a promise. This is passing through the gate or going through a crisis. Please remember that believers must first enter through such a gate of faith, and then they may advance in the walk of faith by maintaining an attitude of faith.

Many people speculate that they can trust God by

maintaining an attitude of faith without ever crossing the threshold of faith by means of a single-minded act of faith. They do not know that without entering the gate there is absolutely no possibility of their walking in the way. Without going through a crisis there can be no opportunity for making progress. It is imperative that there be a clear break with the past and a definite acceptance of the testimony of God. This is entering the gate; otherwise, there can never be any spiritual advancement. Hence in the area of faith, first enter the gate, then walk along the way.

Among the many truths which we have come to believe, there is none higher than that of our being "in Christ." This is the position the redeemed of the Lord obtain, according to the teaching of the New Testament. Nothing can be higher than this position, since the forgiveness of sins is in Christ, justification is in Christ, and sanctification is also in Christ. All spiritual blessings are in Christ. Everything is in Him. So that our being placed in Christ is a higher grace than any other we can ever receive. All that God gives to us is in His Son.

The most important question for us today, then, is how can we be in Christ? The English missionary to China, Hudson Taylor, admired the victorious life, and he knew that all was to be found in Christ. Yet in the beginning of his Christian walk, he struggled to abide in Christ, and found that he could not do so because he often seemed to fall out of Christ. This struggle went on until one day God gave Hudson Taylor a revelation that showed him he was already in Christ. His need was not going to be remedied by his asking to be put in Christ. On the contrary, he was a regenerated person and therefore he was already in Christ. The answer to his need was simply to rest upon this fact, for such was the meaning of abiding in Christ. Since he was already in Christ, he had no way of being more in Him. Thus he entered into victory. And such is the gate of faith. Hudson Taylor now entered the gate. And after such an entry by the act of faith, he could learn to lay hold of this fact day by day and trust God with an attitude of faith. Otherwise, even if he wished to trust in God, he would find no strength to so trust in Him.

Though "in Christ" is such a simple phrase, its truth is exceedingly vast. It is so all-encompassing that it is almost beyond measurement. God "hath blessed us with every spiritual blessing in the heavenly places in Christ" (Eph. 1.3). All the blessings are in Him. Since the blessings in Him are so abundant, why is it that many who seemingly believe do not obtain these blessings? This is because they are ignorant of the two aspects of faith. There must be the act of faith as well as the attitude of faith. Many may have believed and seemingly have exhibited the attitude of faith, yet they lack the act of faith. In other words, they have not crossed the threshold of faith at one time and with singleness of mind believed in God's fact. They mistake the attitude of faith for faith itself. If they pass through the crisis of faith, however, they shall experience many of the blessings in Christ by thereafter maintaining this attitude of faith. This does not mean they obtain everything on the day they pass through the gate. In a sense they do possess all; nevertheless, they have not yet experienced all. It is similar to our entering a garden, wherein all is before our eyes; but we have to walk through this garden to experience everything in it. Upon entry, we may possess all by claiming them all as ours. First the gate, then the way.

When God commanded the children of Israel to cross the river Jordan, He first told Joshua: "Now therefore arise, go over this Jordan, thou, and all this people, unto the land which I do give to them, even to the children of Israel. Every place that the sole of your foot shall tread upon, to you have I given it, as I spake unto Moses" (Joshua 1.2,3). Before they crossed the Jordan, God had said He had given the land of Canaan to them. They simply needed to go over and possess. Did they have faith? They *did* have faith, for those who did not believe had already died in the wilderness. And all who were now to enter Canaan were people of faith. They crossed the Jordan River by laying hold of God's word. They held on to His word and declared that thereafter the land of Canaan was theirs. Hence they went through the Jordan to possess it.

But after they crossed Jordan, did they immediately possess all the land? Satan will never make such a concession to God's people. The walls of Jericho were tall and the gates of the city were tightly shut. Had we been there in such a situation, we would probably have gone to God and complained, saying: "You said You had given us the land of Canaan. We have crossed the River, but now the walls of Jericho are so tall and the gates of the city are so securely shut. Has not Your word fallen short?" The children of Israel, however, did nothing of the sort. They believed in God's word and laid hold of His promise. They encircled the city once every day till on the seventh day they encircled it seven times; then they shouted, and in response the walls of Jericho collapsed. And thereafter they conquered one city after another. Although they had their failures and they failed to completely drive out the seven tribes of Canaan, they nonetheless took actual possession of more than half the cities in Canaan.

We must exercise faith to possess all the spiritual blessings in Christ, even as the children of Israel had laid hold of God's word in crossing the river Jordan and possessing the land. This matter can also be likened to title deeds which a dying father gives to his son to inherit, with his son needing to find the lands as described in the deeds and then needing to manage his inheritance. The inheritance is his, yet he has not seen it nor managed it. He must therefore go to investigate and subsequently to manage his properties according to what has been written in the deeds. Hence receiving the title deeds can be viewed as an act of faith, that is to say, a crisis; and enjoying the properties of his inheritance according to the deeds can be viewed as the attitude of faith (or trust)—that is to say, progress.

"Go over this Jordan, thou, and all this people," God had said. This, for the people, constituted a crossing the threshold of faith. And after passing through this crisis, they destroyed one city after another according to God's word. This, for the people, was walking in the way of faith. In reading the New Testament, you see that everything in Christ is yours. But if you have not possessed anything, it is because you have not experienced the crisis of faith. Without passing through the threshold of faith, you will never be able to traverse the way of faith, and your spiritual life will make little progress. Even though you have heard much teaching on faith, you will not be profited. You must go through this crisis, saying, "Oh God, I thank You for You have indeed given the land of Canaan to me. This land is mine." You need to possess the land by holding on to the title deeds. You do not go and investigate to determine if the land is truly yours; on the contrary, you go to claim it because it *is* yours.

Taking the title deeds and accepting the blessing which God in Christ has given to you—that is your experiencing the crisis of faith. There may come a day when on the one hand you sense jealousy and pride and lust within you and on the other hand you sense no love nor humility nor gentleness in you. You ask the Lord to deliver you. You ask Him once, twice, many times. Until one day you are given revelation concerning the riches of Christ, and you realize how foolish of you to have asked for deliverance. You are given to hear this word of God: "My grace is sufficient for thee" (2 Cor. 12.9). And thus there is no need to ask, for the Lord says, "I am holiness, I am gentleness, I am full of grace." Everything is in Him. As God shows you the riches in Christ, you pass through a crisis. Then you will experience more and more of the grace in Christ.

T. Austin-Sparks* is a servant of God who has been greatly used in our time. The most precious truth in his entire life is that of his being "in Christ." His life has been completely changed ever since the day his eyes were opened by God to see the riches that are his in Christ. He was made to realize that he had previously become a poor rich man because he had forgotten the exceeding riches which is the believer's inheritance in Christ. Let us realize today that we must all go through this crisis of faith. May God give us the spirit of wisdom and revelation and have our eyes opened to see our union with Christ.

After you have seen your union with Christ, will you never afterwards lose your temper or have jealousy stirred up within you? Is it that hereafter you exhibit only gentleness and love? May I remind you that the devil is as stubborn today as were the Canaanites in their day. He will resist you at every step of your way. Unless you stand in the victory of Christ, you will see defeat. Whoever has not passed through the crisis of faith will never be able to walk the way of faith. Yet once you have your eyes opened to see the riches in Christ, you will immediately be tempted by the devil; he will insinuate as follows: "You say all blessings are in Christ, yet why is it you will still lose your temper and be angry? You say all blessings are yours, but do you have any within you? The revelation you say you received is not true, you are instead deceived. You say God has given you the land of Canaan; if that be the case, then how is it that the walls

*He died in 1970 in London, England.—*Translator*

of Jericho remain so high and the gates remain so tight? How, then, can you believe you can drive out the seven tribes of Canaan? No, what God has said to you is merely empty word. It is better for you to return to the *eastern shore* of the Jordan River!"

Believers must recognize that crossing the Jordan River but not encircling the city of Jericho is only entering the gate of faith without walking in the way of faith. Crossing the Jordan alone without next encircling Jericho will never cause the walls to fall. Entering the gate of faith without walking in the way of faith will not result in spiritual progress. On the contrary, the spiritual experience of every advancing Christian attests to the *footprints* of faith.

Satan will not easily let go and let you take things with you. You have heard that all things are in Christ. But as soon as you arrive home, Satan will say to you, Love is not yours—gentleness is not yours—nothing is really yours. Is it because of Satan's lie that you give in and give up? You ought to act as landlords do, who manage their lands according to their title deeds. Like them, you ought to take care of your land to the full extent of what is described in the deed. You have no need to ask or to strive. All you need to do is take the deed with you and claim it. And in the event of temptation, you simply need to use the Scripture passage suitable for that occasion. If it is temper, use the applicable Scripture in dealing with temper. If it is love, use the appropriate Scripture verses on love. Finding the proper Scriptures you then can declare: "This is my inheritance, therefore I claim it as my own." You notify Satan that he is a liar, so he must depart from you. You exercise your faith, saying, "I live by the grace of Christ. I can be patient and gentle."

Please note carefully, though, that what should be removed is the temper and not faith. The mountain, not faith. It is not for faith to yield, but for the temper to yield. Stand by faith; no wall is too tall that it cannot fall. The children of Israel did not fight with rods. They simply encircled the city on the first day and went home. And for the next five days they did the same thing. In the eyes of the people of Jericho, it was like child's play. On the seventh day, though, they encircled the city seven times, then shouted with faith that the walls of Jericho would fall, and the walls did indeed fall.

A given Christian may have passed through the crisis of faith, but he has not walked in the way of faith. He laments that his temper, his jealousy, his pride, his lust, and all things else are still with him. He does not know what to do. For the moment, please recall this: that first you must see the riches that are yours in Christ. This is entering the gate of faith. But then upon entering, you must stand into your new position by dealing with whatever temptation comes your way—be it pride or jealousy or whatever. You stand in faith and declare that all these temptations must fall. And fall they will. Hallelujah! The children of Israel surrounded the city of Jericho and shouted the shout of faith that the walls of Jericho would fall. From the human viewpoint, such action was plain foolishness. But as they shouted, the city of Jericho fell. Similarly today, if we cry aloud in faith, then our temper, lust, pride and jealousy will likewise fall. Passing through a crisis means seeing all that is ours in Christ. This constitutes the first step of faith. Then lay hold of all that is in Christ, even as you would hold on to a title deed.

"For ye died" (Col. 3.3). God shows you that you are dead; therefore you should not lose your temper. As you by faith believe in what God in His word says, you enter the gate. But then Satan will come immediately and may cause you to lose your temper either through the provocation of your wife or children or fellow-student or whoever it may be. Naturally you will conclude that probably this word "ye died" in the Bible does not apply to you. And thus you trust in your feeling, and your faith vanishes. Suppose, for example, my father bought some land and gave me the deed to it. He tells me to go and manage this estate. So I go to the country where the land is. I meet a vagabond who asks why I am coming there. "I have come to find my father's land," I reply. "This is not your father's land; it is my father's land," the vagabond protests. Now if I at that moment were to doubt my father's word, I probably would return home. But if I say, "No, no, my father has made no mistake; for according to this title deed in my hand, this land is ours," the vagabond would have to go away. Hence, it is either he or I who must go.

Now with us, it is the same way. For God the Father has already given you all blessings in Christ Jesus. And the Bible is the title deed which the Father gives you. If you believe what is written in the Bible, Satan will have to go. How sad that many people are unable to endure Satanic temptations. They give up the word of God and lose their faith. We must therefore receive the word of God not just once but whenever afterwards we are tempted. We must be strong through God's word. This is walking in the way of faith.

Someone may have declared yesterday that in Christ he had overcome his temper. Yet today his pride comes back. He is puzzled over the fact that he did overcome his temper yesterday but he has today become proud again. Can it be that the Biblical word "for ye died" is not totally dependable? No. It merely means that he should walk in the way of faith. After the victory over Jericho, the children of Israel suffered defeat at Ai. If we depend on ourselves, we will fail right away. But by trusting the word of God, we may overcome all enemies. Do not entertain the thought of living leisurely. We must deal with our temper as well as our pride whenever they arise. The fight of faith is inevitable; the way of faith is invaluable. Each step of our way needs to be taken with "the sole" of faith (see again Joshua 1.3).

A gate and a way—these are the principles of spiritual living. Formerly I had no idea what "all spiritual blessings in Christ" meant. Today I see it. It is passing through a crisis. But after the crisis gate has been entered I need to walk step by step on the ground of what God's word has shown me. This is walking in the way. Both the gate and the way must be taken into account. Without going through the gate, none can walk in the way. Yet by the same token, if the gate is experienced but a person is too lazy to walk, he can make no progress. He must walk step by step and capture city after city with singleness of mind. The enemy will never surrender without a fight. We must fight the spiritual battle.

Obedience

In this matter of obedience, even as in that of faith just discussed, there are also both the gate and the way. First enter the gate of obedience, then walk the way of obedience. Once a few sisters told me that for them obedience was most difficult. Other sisters, they said, seemed to be able to obey easily, but for them to do so, it was like bearing the sufferings of the entire world. My answer to them was this: if you have never entered the gate of obedience, how can you walk in the way of obedience? Let me say here and now that if you have never laid down your will and surrendered to God with singlemindedness, if you have never cast aside what you treasure most and denied what you like best, it is futile for you to think of walking in the way of obedience. If a person remains outside the gate, it is a waste of effort trying to persuade him to obey the Lord. Lead him first through the gate, and then help him to obey God one item after another, thus assisting him in the walk of obedience.

Have you ever once said goodbye to your past? Have you ever once cut out your hardness of heart? Have you ever once denied your quest for self-glory? Unless you have had such a definite experience, you will not be able to walk in the way of obedience because you have not entered its gate yet.

When Rebecca was asked if she would go with the steward of Abraham, she answered: "I will go" (Gen. 24.58). She thus left her father's house. After leaving her father's house, Rebecca rode on a camel and journeyed through the wilderness. This signifies the way of suffering (the camel here signifies suffering). Only thus could she have helped Isaac and pleased him. All Christians should tell the Lord: "Henceforth I am willing to lay down everything, including any person, event or thing, for Your sake." Otherwise, when God says to us today to forsake a certain thing, we shall reply that we cannot for it is too painful. Tomorrow if He would challenge with another matter, we could again respond with: "No, I cannot because that is too painful." It may appear that God is very hard on us. Why? Because we have never left our father's house. "Forget also thine own people, and thy father's house: so will the king desire thy beauty" (Ps. 45.10, 11). In the course of obedience, a Christian, like a virgin who is to be married, must first depart from his father's house and remove himself from his father's protection. Had we thus made such a decision before, we would be able to walk in the way of obedience.

I often say that many people have never suffered as Christians because God has never required it of them. Some Christians do suffer, but they are not happy about it. They have not learned. We ought to be sufficiently joyful in suffering. In case you are still ignorant of what God requires of you or what He expects of you, if you do not know what God's attitude is towards certain matters concerning you, then you have not yet entered the gate of obedience. There must be a time when you say to God with singlemindedness: "Oh God, hereafter I am willing to lay aside my own idea, expectation, ambition and plan. I will cut them off for Your sake." Otherwise, God will not make any request of you. Could Isaac have made request of an unfamiliar woman had Rebecca not yet been married to him? God will not ask you for a penny if you have not yielded yourself to Him with singleness of heart. You may give offerings for the sake of your conscience, but you have not been asked of God.

Let all of us remember that if we expect to walk in the way of obedience, we must pass through the crisis of consecration. Whether we are brothers or sisters, we will make no spiritual progress without consecration. It is imperative that we be disarmed by God. We should not dream of walking in the way of obedience if we have never walked through the gate of obedience. When we are redeemed, we no doubt belong to God. But beginning from the moment of our consecration we shall *experience* that we really do belong to Him.

Is there anyone who has not consecrated himself yet? Have you obeyed because God has touched you on this matter? Are you afraid of His demand? Perhaps the very matter of which you are afraid is that which God requests of you. Whatever you dare not think or touch, whatever you tend to avoid may very well be the matter about which God will speak to you. Oftentimes the Holy Spirit works in you, but you dare not consider; instead, you try to escape. You think of other things, you talk of other things. You may even go read the Bible in order to flee from His voice. Some people flee away when God calls them to preach the gospel. Some people are touched by Him on the matter of money or their relationship with other people or with those in the church. Such divine touch, if accepted, is quite painful to the flesh; yet it is a most blessed touch.

Do not harbor the thought that God does not see the recesses of our hearts. For we are naked and fully exposed before Him. It is best that we say to Him with single-mindedness: "Oh God, hereafter I belong to the Lord Jesus. Hereafter my vision is the Lord Jesus. Hereafter I have nothing to desire on earth but the Lord Jesus." And as we do this, we shall pass through the crisis of obedience. No normal Christian fails to enter this crisis, no good servant of the Lord fails to pass through this gate.

After you have truly entered this gate by consecrating yourself and laying down everything, you then will be tested by the Lord. You will be tested till He is satisfied that you are really His as well as that you are satisfied that you truly are for Him. After Abraham had crossed the River and arrived at Canaan, he was tested by God again and again until finally he offered Isaac. God wanted to prove that Abraham really feared Him. He also wanted Abraham to know that he did fear God. Likewise with us, after we have passed through the crisis, we may have something besides the Lord we still secretly love and admire. If God tells us to deny it, we will deny it if we are faithful. In case we are not so faithful, we will see the cross and by-pass it. There are too many Christians today who take the by-pass. This will only extend the distance of the course. Our course shall be much shorter if we are faithful. It will be longer if we are not faithful, because we will circle around it.

My burden has been to show you that in these two areas of "trust" and "obey," the gate always comes first and then the way follows. Both the gate and the way must be equally stressed. The gate needs to be entered first, then the walk in the way is made possible. Otherwise, all will be in vain, for then all the teachings on faith and obedience will become impractical.

May God bless us today by opening our eyes to see that nothing is too hard for Him, no cost is too great for Him, and no consecration is too much for Him. We believe Him, therefore we enter the gate of faith. We love Him, therefore we enter the gate of obedience. Because He is faithful, we will walk the way of faith. Because He loves, we will tread the way of obedience. "The path of the righteous is as the dawning light, that shineth more and more unto the perfect day" (Prov. 4.18).

2 The Objective and the Subjective

God so loved the world, that he gave his only begotten Son, that whosoever believeth on him should not perish, but have eternal life. (John 3.16)

And I will pray the Father, and he shall give you another Comforter, that he may be with you forever. (John 14.16)

As the branch cannot bear fruit of itself, except it abides in the vine; so neither can ye, except ye abide in me. I am the vine, ye are the branches: he that abideth in me, and I in him, the same beareth much fruit: for apart from me ye can do nothing. (John 15.4b,5)

Even the Spirit of truth: whom this world cannot receive; for it beholdeth him not, neither knoweth him: ye know him; for he abideth with you, and shall be in you. (John 14.17)

Verily, verily, I say unto you, He that believeth hath eternal life. (John 6.47)

Whosoever drinketh of the water that I shall give him shall never thirst; but the water that I shall give him shall become in him a well of water springing up unto eternal life. (John 4.14)

Again, a new commandment write I unto you, which thing is true in him and in you; because the darkness is passing away, and the true light already shineth. (1 John 2.8)

For to me to live is Christ, and to die is gain. (Phil. 1.21)

According to my earnest expectation and hope, that in nothing shall I be put to shame, but that with all boldness, as always, so now also Christ shall be magnified in my body, whether by life, or by death. (Phil. 1.20)

But of him are ye in Christ Jesus, who was made unto us wisdom from God, and righteousness and sanctification, and redemption. (1 Cor. 1.30)

To whom God was pleased to make known what is the riches of the glory of this mystery among the Gentiles, which is Christ in you, the hope of glory. (Col. 1.27)

Two Categories of Truth

The truths to be found in both the New Testament and the Old can be grouped under two categories of truth: the subjective and the objective. For the sake of better understanding, I will first explain what is meant by these two terms. And perhaps the analogy of guest and house owner could be helpful to such understanding. Looking at something from a guest's point of view can be labeled objective; seeing from one's point of view as owner of the house can be labeled subjective. That is objective to the beholder which happens in another's life; that is subjective which happens in one's own life. Hence, all the truths which have not been experienced in one's own life are considered to be objective truths; and all the truths that one *has* experienced in himself are reckoned to be subjective truths. Whatever is outside a person is objective to that person. And yet, though it *is* outside him, it is still truth nonetheless. The Bible lays equal emphasis on both these sides. We can illustrate this matter by means of the following examples.

"God so loved the world, that he gave his only begotten Son" (John 3.16). "And I will pray the Father, and he shall give you another Comforter" (John 14.16). Many people can recite the first of these two passages from memory, but they cannot recite the second. Actually both these passages are equally valuable. God bestows two gifts: in John 3.16 He is said to give us the Son; in John 14.16 He is said to give us the Holy Spirit. God grants His Son to sinners, and the Holy Spirit to all those who believe in His Son. He gives His Son to the world that they may be saved through Him; He gives the Holy Spirit to the believers that they may have the power to overcome. All things done in the Son are objective truths; all things accomplished in me by the Holy Spirit are subjective truths. Accordingly, all that is done in Christ is objective; all that is done in me by the Holy Spirit is subjective.

When Christ died on the cross, I died with Him—and this is an objective fact. Yet if I were to touch myself to find out if I were dead indeed, I would most certainly not feel myself to be dead. When I preach the gospel to a person, telling him that he is a sinner but that Christ has died for him, can he at all possibly see that he did die with Christ? No, for everything in *Christ* is objective to us and outside us. But all the works of the Holy Spirit are wrought in *us*, and therefore they are subjective in nature. The Holy Spirit does nothing within himself but does all in us. Let us therefore remember that whatever is done in Christ is objective and whatever is done in us is subjective.

In John 15.4,5 our Lord mentions "abide in me" twice. What is meant by "abide in me," which phrase, of course, has reference to our being "in Christ"? That which is in Christ, we will recall, is objective. Hence first is mentioned the objective side, and then the subjective experience of "I in [you]." The "I in [you]" follows upon the "abide in me." From this we can see that all subjective experiences are based on objective facts. If there is only the work of the Holy Spirit without the work of Christ, no one can be saved; but neither will anyone be saved if there is only the work of Christ and not the work of the Holy Spirit as well. Just as we are able to stand firmly on our two feet and see clearly with our two eyes, and just as the birds can fly comfortably with their two wings, so we need to abide in Christ and Christ will abide in us.

"He that believeth hath eternal life" (John 6.47). All who believe in the Lord know this. But who can touch the eternal life without Him? It is a matter of faith. In truth, he who believes has eternal life. Yet there is another passage in the Gospel according to

John, which says this: "Whosoever drinketh of the water that I shall give him shall never thirst; but the water that I shall give him shall become in him a well of water springing up unto eternal life" (4.14). This water which the Lord gives is the water of life. It shall become a well of water that shall keep springing up within you so that you may taste its sweetness. John 6.47 presents the objective side which speaks of having eternal life, while John 4.14 presents the subjective side which speaks of tasting eternal life as water which keeps springing up.

It is stated in 1 John 2.8: "which thing is true in him and in you." Some truths are true in Christ, some truths are true in you. Both are truths; and they need to be equally emphasized. How does the Lord speak of bearing fruit? "He that abideth in me, and I in him, the same beareth much fruit" (John 15.5). In other words, when the objective truth maintains equilibrium with the subjective truth (and vice versa), there comes forth much fruit.

The same balance is found in John 14.17, which reads in part: "the Spirit of truth: . . . for he abideth with you, and shall be in you." "Abide with you" is objective in nature. This refers to the presence of Christ being *with* His disciples through the Holy Spirit. "In you," on the other hand, is subjective in nature. This alludes to the indwelling of Christ *in* the disciples by the Holy Spirit. What is now objective, being outside the believer, will become subjective through the indwelling of the Holy Spirit.

Paul declared, on the one hand, that "of [God] are ye in Christ Jesus" (1 Cor. 1.30). On the other hand he declared this: "Christ in you, the hope of glory" (Col. 1.27). Our being in Christ is something objective; Christ being in us is something subjective.

We may discover hundreds of passages in the Bible which speak of both the objective and the subjective realm of truth. By laying hold of these two realms together, we may say we have laid down the tracks of God's word. A train travels on a double track, it being rather dangerous for it to run on a single one; but on a double track it can run safely. Likewise, if we pay equal attention to the objective and subjective sides of Christian truth, we shall not fall into danger but shall be greatly helped. Here I have no intention of discussing theology; I would instead rather speak a little on practical living. Let me mention some of the greatest facts which have been accomplished objectively in Christ, and also their corresponding experiences that are produced subjectively in us through the working of the Holy Spirit.

Fact One

First and foremost is the fact that Christ has died on the cross for our sins. This is the center of all objective truths in the Bible. In reading the Scriptures we will discover everywhere how Christ died, how He atoned for our sins and how He is our propitiation. There on the cross He bore in His body our sins. Redemption has already been accomplished. And this is now a fact.

Since the Lord Jesus has borne the sin of the whole world, why is the whole world not saved?

Moreover, why is it that some who have believed and are saved do not have the joy of salvation? Why do they still worry about their sins? All this is because people only look at the subjective side. How can anyone be saved if all he sees are the sins and uncleanness in himself? We ought to realize that what Christ has done is on the objective side. It cannot be found on the subjective side. For what the Lord has done was done *at Calvary*, not in us. How can we ever find it in us? But the moment we all realize it was on the cross that Christ died for our sins, we will shout, Hallelujah! He has borne our sins, and therefore we can be saved! Whenever faith reaches out to the objective truth, the Holy Spirit will work in people to give them the peace of forgiveness and the joy of salvation. We can never find such solace on the subjective side, because that is not the way of God. God gives first His Son to men, then He gives the Holy Spirit. The bestowing of the Holy Spirit follows the bestowing of the Son. First Christ, and then the Holy Spirit. The Holy Spirit works *in* us all which the Lord has done *outside* us.

The letter to the Hebrews tells us that faith is like "an anchor of the soul, both sure and stedfast and entering into that which is within the veil" (6.19). Suppose we are on a steamer which has a huge anchor. What is the use of the anchor if it stays on the steamer? It is to be cast into the water so as to stabilize the vessel. It is not to stay put on the steamer. Likewise is it with faith. Faith never believes in what is in us; faith casts itself upon the Lord Jesus. It is cast from us to Christ. Whenever faith holds on to the objective, it holds fast to the subjective. If the anchor remains on the steamer, it will not help to stabilize the ship. If there are more anchors on the steamer, will they help in steadying the ship? Let me tell you, should the steamer be loaded with even larger anchors, it will still not be steadied unless those anchors are thrown into the water. The more we look at ourselves, the more disappointed we become. But if we cast the anchor of faith onto the cross of the Lord Jesus we shall have peace. We should always commence with the objective, and then conclude with the subjective. So here are the two sides: we will never be benefited if we only pay attention to the indwelling Holy Spirit without first noticing the finished work of Christ on the cross; yet neither will we have any experience if we look exclusively at what Christ has accomplished on the cross without looking as well at what the Holy Spirit will do in us.

Another case will be this matter of our co-crucifixion with Christ. Do we crucify ourselves? No. "Knowing this, that our old man was crucified with him, that the body of sin might be done away, that so we should no longer be in bondage to sin" (Rom. 6.6). It is not that we crucify ourselves, but that our old man *was* crucified with Christ at the time He himself was crucified. This is an objective fact. Your eyes must be fixed on the Lord. Were you to try to crucify yourself, you would discover how wicked you are and how impossible it is for you to die. The greatest mistake made by believers is right here: although the Bible says that I was crucified with Christ, I look at myself and find myself as hard and corrupted and undisciplined as I ever was. Even so, I try to crucify myself; yet I cannot make myself die. And that is where the mistake begins: you begin with yourself. You should keep in mind, instead, that all real beginnings lie with Christ. You do not die because you have seen yourself dead. You only become dead because you died when Christ died. The anchor is only effective when it is cast forth. Faith is not operative till it is cast towards Christ. How can you make yourself die if you always look at yourself and pretend to die? Let us ever keep in mind that you and I became dead with Christ when He died on the cross. And this is what Christ has done. Objectively, He has died, and hence you too have died.

"If ye live after the flesh, ye must die;but if by the Spirit ye put to death the deeds of the body, ye shall live" (Rom. 8.13). This is a perfect complement to Romans 6.6. There it is speaking of co-crucifixion with Christ; here, however, it speaks of our putting to death the deeds of the body by the Holy Spirit. Crucifixion is that which is finished in Christ; mortification is that which is to be done by the Holy Spirit. To be crucified with Christ is what I believe and is objective. I can shout Hallelujah!, because when Christ died, my old man was crucified with Him. But on the subjective side, if I today am willing to obey by responding affirmatively as the Holy Spirit reminds me that a certain thing has already been crucified, I am dead indeed to that particular thing. Tomorrow the Holy Spirit will mention to me another thing about myself that was already crucified, and it will indeed be crucified experientially if I am willing to let it go. The Holy Spirit tells me my temper has been crucified, and therefore I need not lose my temper; if I say, I am willing not to lose my temper, I will be given strength by the Holy Spirit not to lose it. The Holy Spirit says that my pride has already been crucified, so I have no obligation to be proud; if I say, I am willing not to be proud, I will be granted power by the Holy Spirit not to be. As I am willing to obey in one thing after another, the Holy Spirit will work out God's salvation in me one by one. In case I attempt to suppress my temper by my own effort, however, I will not succeed even if I try my utmost. By looking first at what Christ in His death has done, I find the Holy Spirit is applying that death in me.

During the first two Christian centuries, the believers greeted one another with either "The Lord is coming" or "In Christ." How sweet and precious to be in Christ. And the Holy Spirit in you will put to death the deeds of your body. Today, Christians stress too much either the objective or the subjective truth. Too much emphasis laid on the subjective side will result in self-suppression, which is as futile as not casting the anchor into the water. Yet it will be equally futile if any should be careless in his spiritual walk because he reckons Christ has already died. Christ has indeed died on the cross, but a person will still perish unless he believes—unless he casts the anchor of faith onto Christ. If he is willing to believe in the death of Christ on the cross, he will be saved. In like manner, the Holy Spirit tells you that your temper, your lust, your pride or your jealousy were crucified, and if you are willing to accept this fact, you will be given power by the Holy Spirit to overcome. You on your side believe in the objective truth, and the Holy Spirit on His side will translate what is objective into your subjective experience. You believe in truth outside you, and the Holy Spirit will make it operative within you. You believe in the finished work of Calvary, and the Holy Spirit will make it real in you.

Fact Two

This is not only the case with the truth of co-death; it also is the case with the truth of co-resurrection. "And raised us up with him [Christ]" (Eph. 2.6). How are we raised up? Raised up with Christ. See once again that it is Christ. Once more it is objective fact that we see. "Begat us again unto a living hope by the resurrection of Jesus Christ from the dead" (1 Peter 1.3). In other words, when a person is born again, he is at the same moment raised up with Christ. Every born-again Christian has been resurrected with Christ, and vice versa. Raised with Him, for it is He who has raised us up.

What is meant by resurrection? The Lord Jesus had died. His body was there, but all His blood had drained out. There were numerous wounds in His head due to His having worn the thorny crown; there were nail prints in His hands and feet as well as a spear wound in His side. The power of death had seized His body. But lo and behold, the life of God entered this body and He now lives. This life in the Lord Jesus overcomes all the powers of death and resurrects His body. In death His eyes could not see, His ears could not hear, nor could His hands and feet move. But now He can. Death in the Bible means being absolutely powerless and weak. Death is a spiritual inability and a spiritual impossibility. Previously, Jesus' body had been bound around with layers of linen; what happened, though, at His resurrection? The resurrection of our Lord Jesus was different from that of Lazarus. In Lazarus' case, when he came out of the tomb, his hands and feet were bound with gravecloths and his face was bound about with a napkin. He needed people to loosen him. But in the resurrection of our Lord, the Bible records: "the linen cloths lying, and the napkin, that was upon his head, not lying with the linen cloths, but rolled up in a place by itself" (John 20.6b, 7). He did not need to have the linen cloths and napkin gradually unloosed or cut. As the powerful life of God flowed into Him, both the legitimate and the illegitimate bondages lost their power. Once His body was a corpse; but now it is alive and active. Such is the resurrection of our Lord Jesus.

I recall when I first began to serve the Lord that I prayed He would raise me up with Him. I thought at the time that if the Lord should raise me up with Him I would then have the power to do God's will. It was wrong for me to pray like this, for once again I had started from myself. The Bible says that I have been raised with Christ. This is an accomplished fact. Remember that the more we turn in to look at ourselves, the worse we become. Please understand, here, that it is not that we should not have subjective experience, it is simply that we must first believe in objective truth. Now I can say, "Lord, I thank You for You have already risen, and I have been raised with You." We need first to believe the fact that I am raised from the dead. Yet how am I raised? Is it because I *feel* I am resurrected? No, it is Christ who has raised me up.

We may ask the same about our salvation. When we were yet sinners, did we not hear the gospel wherein was proclaimed that the Lord Jesus had already died for us and that His blood had already been shed for the remission of our sins? We believe, and so we are saved. We do not look at our side to see if we are good enough, we instead look at the other side wherein the Lord has accomplished redemption on the cross. By laying hold of this fact, we receive peace. Were we to look only on the subjective side of the truth without equally applying the objective side, we would not be able "to fly" because we have but "one wing." We must look at one half and not overlook the other half.

Ephesians 2.6 declares that God has "raised us up with him"; whereas Ephesians 1.19,20 declares: "what is the exceeding greatness of his power to us-ward who believe, according to that working of the strength of his might which he wrought in Christ, when he raised him from the dead . . ." Though the believers in Ephesus already knew they were raised up with Christ from among the dead, they were nonetheless urged by the apostle Paul to know the exceeding greatness of the manifested power of God. In other words, though we know resurrection, we need also the *power* of resurrection. On the objective side, there is already resurrection; but on the subjective side, there is still the need of knowing the power of resurrection. No one should say because his temper has been crucified he therefore has lost his temper. On the objective side, his temper was indeed crucified, but on the subjective side he must put to death his temper by the power of the Holy Spirit. Having the objective truth, there must also be the subjective experience.

An unfortunate situation exists today, which is, that people either do not believe in objective truth yet attempt to get subjective experience, or else believe in objective truth but totally ignore subjective experience. According to the word of God, however, without faith people can never be saved, and without obedience they will not be delivered. Faith is towards the finished work of Christ, while obedience is towards the current work of the Holy Spirit. Faith towards Christ and obedience towards the Holy Spirit. How essential are these two elements of faith and obedience.

"That I may know him, and the power of his resurrection" (Phil. 3.10). Paul declared that the one reason for his counting all things as loss was to know the power of resurrection. He did not say to know resurrection because resurrection was known at the moment he believed in the Lord. Rather, on the subjective side, he knew he must forsake all things before he could know the *power* of the resurrection of Christ.

Fact Three

Ascension is the last accomplished objective truth concerning Christ mentioned in the New Testament. The birth, the suffering, the resurrection and the ascension of our Lord are together the greatest of all truths. Concerning this final matter of ascension, I spent many hours when first believing in the Lord trying to figure out how blessed it would be if I could sit in the heavenly places daily and have sins under my feet. But as with flying an airplane, I could not endure for very long up above. I soon fell down. I prayed and prayed, hoping that one day I could sit securely in the heavenly places and break my old record of ascension. One day as I read Ephesians 2.6 (which says, "and raised us up with him, and made us to sit with him in the heavenly places in Christ Jesus"), I began to understand. At the time a Christian is raised together with Christ, he is also made to sit with Christ in the heavenly places. He sits there with Christ not because of his diligence or because of his prayer, but because he was taken to the heavenly places at the time Christ himself ascended to heaven. Christ is in the heavenly places, and therefore I too am in the heavenly places.

Yet I need to allow the power of His ascension to be manifested through me, for on the other hand, in the Bible we also see this: "If then ye were raised together with Christ, seek the things that are above, where Christ is, seated on the right hand of God. Set your mind on the things that are above, not on the things that are upon the earth. For ye died, and your life is hid with Christ in God" (Col. 3.1–3). This is the subjective side of the matter. "Your life is hid with Christ in God"—such is ascension. Since you have died, been raised and ascended, you ought to seek the things above. You ought to think of these things daily. Suppose a sinner, for example, heard that the Lord Jesus has died for his sins. He should not think that since the Lord has died for his sins, he could go on sinning. In spite of the fact that we have the ascended position, we will not be profited by it if we set our mind on the things here below. Only when on the one hand we believe that when Christ ascended we too ascended and on the other hand set our mind on the things above will we truly be in the heavenly places both objectively and subjectively.

Fruit-Bearing

Our having objective fact but not having the corresponding subjective experience approaches the realm of idealism without eliciting any favor from heaven. On the objective side, Christ has done it all; so He must be trusted wholeheartedly. On the subjective side, the Holy Spirit will do the work; and therefore He must be obeyed absolutely. All spiritual experiences commence with our believing what Christ has accomplished, and they conclude with our obeying what the Holy Spirit commands us to do. What Christ has accomplished gives us the position; what the Holy Spirit commands causes us to have experience. What Christ has accomplished is fact that must be received; what the Holy Spirit leads us into is principle which requires our obedience. All spiritual experiences begin from the objective; there is no exception to the rule. The anchor of faith must be cast upon the death, the resurrection, and the ascension of Christ.

"Abide in me, and I in you. As the branch cannot bear fruit of itself, except it abides in the vine; so neither can ye, except ye abide in me. I am the vine, ye are the branches: he that abideth in me, and I in him, the same beareth much fruit: for apart from me ye can do nothing" (John 15.4,5). The order here is very important. First, "in me"—the "me" being Christ. First, abide in Christ. This is objective. Next, "I in him"—that is, Christ abides in you and me. This is subjective. With the objective comes the subjective. And finally, the promise of bearing much fruit. As we believe in the objective fact, we find it is being incorporated into us. And ultimately, the objective plus the subjective shall result in fruit-bearing. Having the objective alone will not produce fruit, yet neither will only having the subjective ever bear fruit. The combination of both these realms brings in fruit.

In the upper room in Jerusalem in the early days after Christ's ascension there were men and women gathered together for prayer. In typology, we can say that man here represents objective truth, while woman represents subjective truth. The presence of men signifies the presence of objective truth, that is to say, the presence of truth is there. The presence of women signifies the presence of subjective truth, which means that the presence of experience is there. And the result of both was that three thousand and later five thousand souls were added to the church

(Acts 2.41; 4.4). That is how the church began. At the time of the second coming of the Lord, there will be on the one hand the Lamb of God—the objective element; and on the other hand, there will be the Bride of the Lamb—the subjective element, who through God's grace shall be clothed, bright and pure, with fine linen—the fine linen being the righteous acts of the saints (Rev. 19.8).

Whether or not a Christian lives to please the Lord depends on whether or not he is balanced in these two sides of the objective and the subjective. Today in the church some specialize on teaching subjective truth, such as the Holiness people; in that case, typologically speaking, you have only the women. Some others, however, are only interested in advocating objective truth, such as the Brethren; and in that case, you have only the men. Both suffer loss. Stressing only the subjective will not produce the right experience; it instead will bring in much unnecessary hardship. On the other hand, emphasizing the objective alone will not produce the corresponding experience either, but will result in self-deception. Hence the unbalanced attention paid to either is not God's way. According to the principle of the Bible, the order is first the objective, then the subjective. First the fact of Christ, then the leading of the Holy Spirit. And the result is bearing much fruit.

May God enable us to know how to obey and serve Him more in His way.

3 Work In and Work Out

So then, my beloved, even as ye have always obeyed, not as in my presence only, but now much more in my absence, work out your own salvation with fear and trembling; for it is God who worketh in you both to will and to work, for his good pleasure. Do all things without murmurings and questionings; that ye may become blameless and harmless, children of God without blemish, in the midst of a crooked and perverse generation, among whom ye are seen as lights in the world, holding forth the word of life; that I may have whereof to glory in the day of Christ, that I did not run in vain neither labor in vain. Yea, and if I am offered upon the sacrifice and service of your faith, I joy, and rejoice with you all: and in the same manner do ye also joy, and rejoice with me. (Phil. 2.12–18)

We all know that the letter to the Philippians was written by Paul in a Roman prison. He wrote not only this letter from there but also the letters to the Ephesians and to the Colossians. Each of these three letters he wrote has its own emphasis. The one to the Ephesians speaks on the church as being the body of Christ; the one to the Colossians speaks of what Christ is to the church. But the one to the Philippians does not deal with such deep doctrines as found in the other two letters; it instead shares, among other things, some personal words of Paul on ending a contention between two sisters in the Philippian church: "I exhort Euodia, and I exhort Syntyche, to be of the same mind in the Lord" (4.2). These two serving sisters were at odds with each other, so Paul gave them a special exhortation.

The letter to the Philippians pays particular attention to humility, peace, and mutual love. It can be said that this epistle is a kind of commentary on First Corinthians chapter 13. Paul in chapter 2 of his letter admonishes the Philippian believers to be in lowliness of mind, each counting the other better than himself; not looking each to his own things but also to the things of others. He followed up such admonitions with the example of the Lord Jesus and how he emptied himself, taking the form of a servant, being made in the likeness of a man, and how He humbled himself, becoming obedient to death, even that of the cross. He told them that such was the mind of Christ which they too ought to have.

Yet with such a word as this, a problem immediately arises. Though the heart is willing, the power to comply is absent. To listen is one thing, to do is another. As the apostle Paul spoke of how the Lord emptied himself and humbled himself—becoming obedient to death, even the death of the cross—the two contentious sisters might likely think, How can we possibly arrive at such a high and noble place? And for this reason, Paul continued to write further in chapter 2 and with verses 12 to 18 in order to show them how this could be achieved.

"So then, my beloved, even as ye have always obeyed, not as in my presence only, but now much more in my absence, work out your salvation with fear and trembling" (v.12). "So then" indicates a continuation in the mind of the writer of what precedes it. "My beloved" is a title which Paul uses whenever he is going to mention something of vital importance. "Even as ye have always obeyed, not as in my presence only, but now much more in my absence." What is the meaning of these words? Paul meant that when he formerly preached the gospel in their midst they had always been obedient to him; and now that there is a problem they should be even more obedient to him: you were obedient to me not only when I preached the gospel in your midst, not only when I was an example to you while with you, and not only when you were in constant contact with me; but you are going to be obedient to me even now. These words therefore include three things: (1) you were obedient to me when I was with you because you were in contact with me; (2) you should be even more obedient now that I am not with you, for I have committed you entirely to God; and (3) one thing you must now obey and perform, which is, to work out your salvation with fear and trembling.

"Work out your own salvation with fear and trembling." Let us read this word many times. "Fear" is towards God while "trembling" is towards oneself. We must fear God on the one hand, we must tremble towards ourselves on the other. God is so high, and hence we must fear Him. Temptation is so severe, and so we must tremble at ourselves. But how is this work of salvation to be worked out? We thank God, for He has a way to work it out.

The Bible divides the matter of salvation into three periods. The first period is the past when God saved us from the penalty of sin which is hell. The second period is the present in which God is saving us from the power of sin. The third period is the future when God will save us from the presence of sin to enter the kingdom and to reign with Christ. Let me illustrate each of them with a pertinent verse:

(1) "Who [God] *saved* us, and called us . . ." (2 Tim. 1.9). This is the past experience which everyone who believes has had.

(2) "Wherefore also [Christ] is able to save to the *uttermost* them that draw near unto God through him . . ." (Heb. 7.25). This is present salvation which we may obtain today.

(3) "So Christ also, having been once offered to bear the sins of many, shall appear a second time, apart from sin, to them that wait for him, *unto salvation*" (Heb. 9.28). This is future and complete salvation.

Thus it is evident that the Scriptures speak of these three periods of salvation. All Christians may have the salvation past, but they may not have the salvation present and future. Some may have the salvation past and present, and they are looking for the salvation future. A person may be saved from the penalty of hell, yet he may still sin daily. A person may be saved from the penalty of hell, but he may not necessarily reign in the future.

I will quote three more Scriptures to prove the validity of these three periods of salvation.

(1) "By grace have ye been saved . . ." (Eph. 2.8). This refers to salvation past.

(2) "If, while we were enemies, we were reconciled to God through the death of his Son, much more, being reconciled, shall we be saved by his life" (Rom. 5.10). This speaks of how we now are saved by the Lord's life.

(3) "In hope were we saved" (Rom. 8.24). This points to the future salvation.

We thank and praise God, for we were saved! Nevertheless, there are two periods of salvation yet to be experienced. Hence we must earnestly pursue. To people who have not been saved, we should tell them to believe that they may be saved from the penalty of hell. But to us who are saved from hell, we need to be saved from the power of sin, as well as to seek after the glory of the kingdom to come. Let us accordingly work out our own salvation with fear and trembling.

Dwight L. Moody was a powerful evangelist, most wise in saving souls. He once said that in his whole life he had never seen a lazy person saved! It seems, therefore, that if a person is lazy, he may not even be delivered from the punishment of hell. "Wherefore he saith, Awake, thou that sleepest, and arise from the dead, and Christ shall shine upon thee" (Eph. 5.14).

Some time ago, I spoke on how we could do nothing to earn salvation from the penalty of hell. If we were to try to work for that, I said, it would be most agonizing. We need only to surrender and to believe, I affirmed, for Christ has done everything for us. All that is indeed true. Yet it is only one half of the truth. The other half is that we must work out our own salvation with fear and trembling. This is something for which we ourselves must take responsibility. If we do not take the responsibility, we shall be lopsided in our Christian life. Christ has indeed died for us, shed His blood for us, been resurrected and ascended for us. Yet some people infer from this that such being the case, they have nothing to do but to worship. And thus they become absolutely passive. They feel no need for prayer or Bible reading or consecration. Let it be known, however, that since God has done all for us, we need to be even more zealous. Because God has already worked in, we must work it out. How are we able to work it out? The next verse in Philippians 2 tells us how.

"For it is God who worketh in you both to will and to work, for his good pleasure" (v.13). Philippians 2.12 and 2.13 show us the two sides of the one glorious truth. Considering verse 12, it would seem as though *we* have to do everything; but in considering verse 13, it would appear that *God* will do everything. One says *we* must work, the other says *God* will work. These two are not contradictory, rather they are complementary. For although verse 12 does indeed say we must work, verse 13 tells us that God will *enable us* to do what we ought to do.

These two verses go a long way in explaining to us a most important fact concerning the two sides of truth in Scripture. We see in the Bible the one side of God's many solemn commandments which He commands us to do as though He were putting an unbearable burden upon us. Not having the strength to bear it all, we are almost crushed under such burden. But we also see in God's word the other side of the many promises of the Lord: how He does everything, how all is of grace and all is of His work—it would appear we need not do anything. Now those individuals who do not perceive and understand these two sides of truth shall no doubt fall onto the one side or the other. One class of people will think that since these are God's commandments, they must do them by themselves. And consequently they look at them as heavy burdens which they must bear and yet cannot bear. They very likely will be completely crushed. Another class of people will view all as being God's grace and all as being His work, and hence they will have not the slightest sense of responsibility. And as a result, they become very loose in their Christian walk.

To be lopsided—disregarding which side one falls on—is perilous. It will result in neither keeping the commandments of God nor in obtaining the promises of God, because the truth of God is well balanced and stresses both sides equally. God works in, and we work out. If we only allow God to work His salvation into us and refuse to work it out, we will get nothing. Or if we try to work salvation out without God having worked it into us first, we will likewise accomplish nothing.

All the affairs of human life are summed up in the phrase "to will and to work." "To will" is the inward decision, while "to work" is the outward action. Whatever is inwardly decided is worked out outwardly. So that to will points to our heart condition and to work refers to our outward living. Nevertheless, whether we will inwardly or work outwardly, it is God who works in us till we accomplish His good pleasure. All our decisions come from the working of God, and all our actions are dependent on the working of God.

How frequently we intend on obeying God, yet we cannot. But God says: I work in you, therefore you can obey. Many Christians feel most miserable because they cannot do many things. Often we tell God: "It is so hard to obey You. I just cannot do it. For me to not love the world is an impossibility. It is equally difficult for me to not hate a certain person." Nevertheless, God does not want you to suffer. He works in you so as to enable you to obey His will. For this reason, you ought to say to God: Although I cannot obey, neither can I forsake the world, nor love people, I nonetheless ask You to so work in me that I may be willing to obey You, forsake the world, and love people. If you pray believing, you will be transformed. What you were unable to overcome in the last three or four years, you will overcome by simply committing and believing.

When Robert Chapman began to serve the Lord, his audience kept increasing. A big church building was put up. D. L. Moody heard of his fame, so he took the train one day and went to hear Chapman. He sat there quietly listening. When the meeting was over, Chapman recognized Moody and came to him to ask him to speak frankly if he had anything to say. "Brother," said Moody, "what you did was a failure and not a success because there is something wrong in your life." Upon hearing this, Chapman was rather unhappy. He felt Moody should not have criticized him in such a way, for what authority did Moody have to speak to him thus? Nevertheless, Moody had said it, and Chapman himself knew that there was in truth some imperfection in himself. He knew he could not give up his wife and children, and over this matter he struggled painfully during the next several weeks. Finally, he told God: "God, I cannot help loving my wife and children, but I ask You to work in me till I am able to give them up." From that day onward, he came to know how to really love his wife and children in the Lord. And from that moment Robert Chapman became very powerful in service. Once he was asked to give his testimony, and he spoke these words: "If there is any ability in me, I know where it comes from. It comes from that obedience."

God will work in us till we are able to work. For example, the man who was wounded by robbers on the way to Jericho was set by the Samaritan on his own beast and brought to an inn. We would like to walk but we have no strength because we have been wounded by sin. We ourselves can never have the strength to walk. Nevertheless, God works in us, really enabling us to will and to work out our own salvation. Whatever accomplishes the good pleasure of God is the result of His working in us both to will and to work. We would do well to remember this.

D. M. Panton of England had this word to say: "Because God dwells in me, I can do all things that God himself can do." A lady once died, and on the tombstone were inscribed her own words: "She did what she could not do!"

Daily we live through impassable days. For us to obtain perfect salvation and live a clean life, it *has* to be the work of God. Many try to imitate Christ, which they will never succeed in doing. Yet because God does it, I can do it. Hold fast to the fact that He works in me. It is not I who work; I only work because God is first working. If I ever attempt to work out the lofty demands of the Bible by myself, I am destined for failure. All I must do is to ask God to work in me till I am willing.

The same Mr. Panton referred to earlier has told this story. Once a physician sent a nurse to tell a patient to do a certain thing. The nurse told the patient what the doctor had ordered, but the patient replied that he could not do it. The nurse reported back to the physician what he had said. So the physician went himself to examine the man in order to find out why he did not do as ordered. What the doctor found out was neither because the patient could nor would not, but because the patient could not *will*. Inside us we will not, and therefore outside us we cannot. Inwardly we will not forsake the world, outwardly we cannot forsake it. But God is able to work in us both to will and to work out His good pleasure.

Because God has worked in, we can work out. Since He has already worked in us, we ought to work it out. So that what we will now stress is the matter of how we can work God's salvation out. Not waiting, not praying, but actually the working out of it now. All who have believed in the Lord have Christ Jesus dwelling in them. "Know ye not as to your own selves, that Jesus Christ is in you? unless indeed ye be reprobate" (2 Cor. 13.5).

There are two common errors in the thinking of many Christians: one is that I must do good, I expect to be good, and I hope to live a spiritual life; the other is that since I have been saved, I do not need to lift a finger in terms of prayer, reading the word of God, or consecrating myself—because Christ himself will make me zealous. The error of the first lies in trying to do good by depending on one's own self; the error of the second lies in the attitude of not seeking earnestly at all. The fact of the matter is that if a person is not diligent after he is saved from hell's penalty he will not live a spiritual life; but then too, neither will he be successful if he does not believe and depend on God. One must believe that it is God who works in him both to will and to work so that he may pray and read the Bible and bear witness. To believe comes first, and then the working out. The kingdom of heaven is to be entered by violence, and the violent take it by force (Matt. 11.12). Day by day we must diligently work out our own salvation. This is not an impossible thing because God has already worked in us. Since we have already obtained, we certainly are able. Let me give an illustration.

"Take heed to yourselves," said the Lord to His disciples; "if thy brother sin, rebuke him; and if he repent, forgive him. And if he sin against thee seven times in the day, and seven times turn again to thee, saying, I repent; thou shalt forgive him" (Luke 17. 3,4). As soon as He finished uttering this word, the disciples instantly prayed: "Increase our faith" (v.5). They knew that this one particular thing they could never possibly do in themselves. To forgive once, twice or thrice was something they were probably sufficiently equipped in themselves to perform. But to forgive seven times in one day was just *too* much. Who could be that patient in the face of such provocation? And hence they asked the Lord to increase their faith. How did He answer them? "And the Lord said, If ye have faith as a grain of mustard seed, ye would say unto this sycamine tree, Be thou rooted up, and be thou planted in the sea; and it would obey you." What relationship is that word of the Lord's to forgiving? Well, because you have faith within you, you can say to your heart of hate: Hate, I command you to leave me. Having such kind of faith, you can certainly forgive people when they ask for it. Believing God has done it, you too are able to do it. Not just in forgiveness, but likewise in prayer, in reading God's word and in not loving the world, faith must first be present. You are able because you believe God makes you able.

"Do all things without murmurings and questionings" (v.14). The apostle has already told them that it is God who works in them both to will and to work. The result of such working is most evident in that there will be peace without either fretfulness or friction. There will be no questioning for there is no doubting; no murmuring, for there is faith and love. Verse 13 speaks of the life of God working in me; verse 14 tells of the perfect harmony which can result.

Such manifestation is found not only in Philippians but also in Ephesians and Colossians. After Ephesians 3.19 speaks of how "ye may be filled unto all the fulness of God" (verses 20–21 being the words of a doxology), chapter 4.2–3 immediately afterwards dwells on "all lowliness and meekness, with longsuffering, forbearing one another in love; giving diligence to keep the unity of the Spirit in the bond of peace." As the power of God works within, peace and harmony are seen among believers. "Strengthened with all power, according to the might of his glory, unto all patience and longsuffering with joy" (Col. 1.11). The might of His glory is the greatest of God's power. Having obtained such glorious might, we are able to perform a rather miraculous feat beyond any human expectation: "unto all patience and longsuffering with joy" is the greatest manifestation of the power of God. To be patient with a troublesome believer is more difficult than to pray and receive an answer from God. It is hard to be patient, but the power of God enables us to do so. In all three Pauline letters, we see that when a Christian receives the working and the filling of the power of God, he is able to be at peace with people as well as to be patient and forbearing.

"That ye may become blameless and harmless, children of God without blemish, in the midst of a crooked and perverse generation, among whom ye are seen as lights in the world" (v.15): "blameless" because people have nothing to speak of against you; "harmless" because there is simplicity and singleness of mind within you. "Crooked" means not straight, while "perverse" means out of joint. In this generation which is twisted and out of joint towards the will of God, a Christian is quite different because he is simple and blameless. He shines as a light in this world. Such is a manifestation of life.

"Holding forth the word of life; that I may have whereof to glory in the day of Christ, that I did not run in vain neither labor in vain" (v.16). Some believers think they do not need to open their mouths and testify as long as they maintain good conduct to attract people to the Lord. But these are ignorant believers. We need to testify with our mouths as well as with our life. We must hold forth the word of life. We must bring out the word of life and lift it up for people to see. The Bible never implies we can testify only with our life and not with the lips as well. We should open our mouth to testify among our relations, friends, and those with whom we are in contact. Otherwise we will not be able to hold forth the word of life. It is true that Jesus in the Gospel of Matthew says, "Ye are the light of the world" (5.14); but in the same Gospel He also declares: "Every one therefore who shall confess me before men, him will I also confess before my Father who is in heaven" (10.32). If you are able to believe and to do, then believe also that you can shine with your life and testify with your mouth in the midst of those among whom you live. In so doing, Paul says you are perfect.

"The day of Christ" refers to the day when He shall reign. The word "run" in the phrase "run in vain" refers to seeking out sinners and preaching the gospel. And "labor" in "labor in vain" refers to serving the believers—shepherding and teaching them. The apostle considers himself as not running or laboring in vain if the believers can be seen as lights in the world.

"Yea, and if I am offered upon the sacrifice and service of your faith, I joy, and rejoice with you all" (v.17). "The sacrifice and service of your faith" reflects the same thought as is found in the words "present your bodies a living sacrifice" in Romans 12.1. What Paul means here in Philippians is simply this: if you Philippian believers will present yourselves as a living sacrifice, I am willing to pour out my life as a libation.

"I joy, and rejoice with you all"—Paul is joyous, and he will rejoice with them all.

"And in the same manner do ye also joy, and rejoice with me" (v.18). The preceding verse mentions how *Paul* is joyful and that he will rejoice with them all. Verse 18 says *they* are joyful and therefore rejoice with him. Oh, those who are truly moved by the power of God have nothing but joy.

We believe God has already worked, and therefore we also can work. All shall be well if we now are willing.

4 Rest Given and Rest Found

Come unto me, all ye that labor and are heavy laden, and I will give you rest. Take my yoke upon you, and learn of me; for I am meek and lowly in heart; and ye shall find rest unto your souls. For my yoke is easy, and my burden is light. (Matt. 11.28–30)

By reading the entire Scripture passage from Matthew 11.20–30, we can perceive that the Lord Jesus is expressing His inward feeling. Before He uttered these words, He had suffered great provocation. He was greatly provoked by the fact that in spite of His doing many mighty works in Chorazin, Bethsaida and Capernaum such as healing many sick people and helping many needy ones, the response He received was an unrepentant spirit. Notwithstanding what they had heard and seen, which testified to them that the Lord Jesus indeed came from heaven to be their Savior and Messiah, they would not believe. They might have given lip service to the Lord, yet their hearts remained hard and unrepentant. All that the Lord had done seemed to be in vain. Hence, Matthew records for us here the prayer of our Lord Jesus Christ.

Let us notice the first words of Matthew 11.25: "At that season." Our Lord prayed His prayer under this kind of circumstance. He prayed to His Father, saying, "I thank thee, O Father, Lord of heaven and earth that thou didst hide these things from the wise and understanding, and didst reveal them unto babes." The people in these larger communities regarded themselves as "the wise and understanding," and thus they could not bring themselves to accept the Lord Jesus. Though our Lord would like to have seen them saved, He loved even more to obey the will of God. Although He was rejected by them, He could nonetheless say to God, "I thank thee, O Father, . . . that thou didst hide these things from the wise and understanding, and didst reveal them unto babes" (v.25). Under a most difficult situation which normally would cause deep despair, He honored God's will and deemed it His great joy. He ignored His own thought by saying, "Yea, Father, for so it was well-pleasing in thy sight" (v.26). He did not say, "Nay," He instead said, "Yea." He could say at any time, "Yea, Father." For He was always mindful of the good pleasures of the Father. He knew full well the substance of the next verse: "All things have been delivered unto me of my Father: and no one knoweth the Son, save the Father; neither doth any know the Father, save the Son, and he to whomsoever the Son willeth to reveal him" (v.27). People in the bigger towns might not know the Son nor repent; nonetheless, His heart was satisfied.

Here reveals the secret of the inward peace of our Lord under any kind of circumstance. He could rest on the basis of His relationship with the Father. As long as the Father knew, all was well with Him. The approval and the praise of His Father was all He sought after; He could not care less about the treatment He received from men. The Father's smile and the Father's will were sufficient for Him; He would not be mindful of the consequence of the world.

Before He had prayed, He found himself in a hard position. He suffered deep misunderstanding. Though He poured out all He had upon the people, He was not well received, and this for no good reason. If you and I had found ourselves in a similar situation, we would probably have called down fire from heaven to burn the people up, even as John and James had once asked be done. We would also have reflected upon the reason or reasons why we had been put into such hard circumstances. We would have murmured and fretted. But our Lord, after He had suffered all these things, said: "Yea, Father, for so it was well-pleasing in thy sight." We would no doubt have been confused and unhappy in such straits. Yet our Lord said, "I thank thee, O Father." His heart was not disturbed at all. In verse 27, He told us the secret of His peace. The preceding verses tell us of the background and how the Lord could rest and remain unmoved by such a situation. But now in verses 28 and 29 He will cause us to see that if we should encounter similar treatment we too can find rest and remain unaffected. We therefore wish at this time to concentrate on these two verses and to perceive how verse 28 and verse 29 speak of two different rests—the one being deeper than the other.

The Rest of Salvation

"Come unto me, all ye that labor and are heavy laden, and I will give you rest" (v.28). This is the rest of salvation. But the one in verse 29 is the rest of victory. The first is that of reconciliation with God; the second is the inward rest of the soul. The first is the rest of salvation while the second is the rest in this world.

"Come unto me, all ye that labor and are heavy laden." How do you feel about the world? Many who have not yet lived a long life have already tasted the bitterness of this world. Such may say, "The world is feverish." When I notice people rubbing shoulders a great deal on a busy street, I begin to wonder what they are so busily occupied with. What are they doing? Are they mad? I do pity them. Let me declare to you that the world is indeed feverish. People have no rest. The Lord does not say, "Come unto me, all ye great sinners, and I will give you rest." The pleasure of sin is sweet, and sinners are anticipating even more pleasure; hence the Lord presents a far different description by saying, "Come unto me, all ye that labor and are heavy laden, and I will give you rest." You labor and you are heavy laden. Although many may enjoy the pleasure of sin, every one senses he is struggling in toil. Many may not sense the pain of sin, yet all acknowledge their life experiences are quite painful. Regardless whether one is a millionaire, a politician, or scholar, a student, a merchant, or a commoner, a laborer or even a beggar, he is not at all satisfied.

Sometimes I think it is quite reasonable for a rikisha man to sigh, but would a millionaire sigh too? Once I stayed in a millionaire's home, and I heard him sigh. Though there are pleasures of sin, life is nonetheless toilsome. On another occasion I was talking with an illiterate woman who exclaimed to me how unfortunate she was because she could not read; otherwise, she asserted, she would believe in Christ and read the Bible. I muse that it is but natural for an illiterate woman to sigh, yet it would not seem possible for a college professor to do so. Who knows that a college professor also sighs! There was once a college professor from abroad who, being very pessimistic, always sighed. On a particular day when the sun was shining brightly and the sky was azure blue, when the grass was very green and the birds on the campus were singing, some of his colleagues said to him, "Sir, observe what a beautiful day it is; certainly you will not sigh *today!*" He looked at the sky and the things around him, and indeed, there was nothing for him to moan about. But what did he say finally? "Alas, such a time does not last long!"

Everywhere you can see people who are laboring greatly and are also heavy laden. They have no rest. They wonder, too, where it will all end. But I am afraid you who read these words may also be toiling without rest. How many of you feel you are burdened beyond measure and have no rest!

Once I went to a village to preach, and there I learned the lesson of being heavy laden. The village I visited was on the other side of a hill, and was inaccessible by train or steamboat. I therefore took a steamboat to a certain point and from there walked uphill and then down to reach it. The day was hot. I carried with me many gospel booklets, pamphlets, some food and extra clothing. I had to transport them myself since I could not find anyone to carry them for me. I felt fine with the first twenty steps, but afterward I could hardly bear the burden. I thought if I could only arrive at my destination quickly I then could rest. But there was no tree on the hill to shade me from the hot sun. And at that moment I began to understand how sinners must labor and how they must be heavy laden. Some of you may not have yet believed in the Lord Jesus; you therefore have no rest. Where, then, are you headed? Listen to the words of the Lord Jesus: "Come unto me, all ye that labor and are heavy laden, and I will give you rest."

This world is in truth a wearisome place. Many have money, but they confess they are tired. Many are in business; they also feel tired. Many possess fame and affection that the world gives, and they too are weary. If they cannot obtain what they seek for, they cannot rest. They know rest is good, but their burden is too heavy. They dare not ask for rest; they can only hope their burden will be lightened. Just like the Israelites in the ancient time who only expected to have their burden *lightened* by Pharaoh instead of expecting total rest from their burden. The condition of the Israelites may represent the condition of the people today. As they had only hoped for their burden to be lightened but not lifted, so men today ask merely for a lighter burden and less worry. Let me declare that what the Lord Jesus Christ gives is not less labor but total rest. Do you know what rest is? It means a ceasing from work. You who are bound by sins and pressed with many burdens have no rest. Then know that the Lord Jesus came to give you rest. You need not do anything; He will simply give it to you.

When I was young, my parents often told me how the Lord Jesus had come to be our Savior by propitiating the wrath of God. I imagined how much good work I must do before God would stop hating me and be willing to save me. Many people think the same way. But please note that the Lord Jesus says here: you do not need to do anything; you may simply come and obtain rest. Jesus does not command you to try hard in doing good, He will simply give you rest. Rest is something men desire, and yet they always assume they must do good before they can be accepted by God. The Lord Jesus, however, calls men to come and receive rest and not to work. As the Scriptures make clear, He has accomplished all works—be they in the area of eternal life, redemption, judgment, justification, or whatever; the Lord Jesus has done them all. Hence now He invites you to come and obtain rest.

Let me tell you another story. In a certain village a Christian was neighbor to an unbelieving carpenter. The Christian knew the truth, and so he frequently attempted to persuade his neighbor to believe in Jesus. The carpenter, however, was obsessed with the idea that in spite of the fact that Jesus had accomplished the work of redemption, he must do good and reform himself before he could believe. No doubt Jesus did atone for his sins; nevertheless, he thought, he still needed to do something. For this reason, the carpenter did not believe.

One night a thief came to the Christian's home and tried to get in through the front door. The thief heard some noise in the house, and so he dared not enter the home but instead stole the door. The next morning the Christian found that his front door had been stolen! He asked his neighbor the carpenter to make another one for him. Being neighbor and friend, the carpenter chose the best material and rushed to finish the work on the same day. But when he was ready to install the door, the Christian, with a serious face, said to him: "Your door is not finished yet; it is not good enough." This naturally embarrassed the carpenter and made him very angry. He said to the Christian: "I chose the best material and rushed to finish the work. Tell me why it is not well done, tell me what I should do to make it good." "Go home and bring some pieces of wood, some nails, and the hammer. I will then show you what to do," answered the Christian.

The carpenter went home and brought the materials asked for. With the hammer, the Christian nailed at random the various pieces of wood onto the door. This made the carpenter even more angry. He thought his Christian neighbor must have lost his mind. Then the Christian began to explain, saying, "Friend, do not be angry at me. Let us talk. Did you indeed finish your door?" "Of course, I did!" answered the carpenter. "But does it not look better by my putting on these extra pieces of wood?" asked the Christian. "The door is already finished," responded the carpenter, "and you only spoil the work by nailing these additional pieces on!" So the Christian in reply said this to him: "The redemptive work of Christ has already been accomplished. In John 19.30 Jesus cried out from the cross: 'It is finished.' But you insist on saying that though the Lord Jesus has indeed done the work, you still want to add something more to it, to improve and to repair it. And so it was because of such reasoning that I decided to nail these pieces of wood to the door which you had finished." With this explanation by the Christian neighbor the carpenter now understood, and he immediately believed in the finished work of the Lord. Yesterday the Christian lost a door, but today God gained a sinner.

The Lord Jesus calls us to obtain rest without any labor because He has already borne our sins, died for us, and been raised from the dead that He might give us a new position before God. We do not need to do anything but merely go to Him for rest. This is the gospel.

Many people in the world labor under a heavy burden. Even in the matter of salvation, they are unable to think otherwise. They believe if they try their best to do good and suffer for it, God may have mercy upon them and save them. Oh, how many such people in Hinduism are doing just this! They lie on beds studded with nails that are pointed upward. They speculate that the unknown god may pity them because of their suffering and forgive their sins. Even our children think that way. Once a child said this: the first thing I did after I sinned was to inflict great pain on myself so that God would forgive my sin.

Oh, the whole world thinks in this fashion: to toil and suffer to whatever degree required so that God will forgive. But please understand that this is a lie, a self-deception, a way of thinking which is totally unrealistic. None can have rest before God through more labor and more burden. Today the call is: "Come unto me, all ye that labor and are heavy laden, and I will give you rest." This is because the work of redemption is finished, the Lord has borne our sins. Whosoever will may come to the Lord and receive rest. No sinner can obtain it by himself. Only by coming to the Lord can he have rest.

The Rest of Victory

I will now speak, and this time to believers, about another rest: "Take my yoke upon you, and learn of me; for I am meek and lowly in heart: and ye shall find rest unto your souls." This rest is what a Christian ought to find. The first rest is what a sinner must have; he will not achieve that rest until he is accepted by God. But a believer has his sins already forgiven. He can rest because the problem of salvation is already solved. Yet sometimes, in spite of having the problem of justification and eternal life resolved, he still has no rest. True, the believer has rested in the Lamb and in His precious blood; nevertheless, he at times finds no rest in his life on earth. Something seems to be disturbing him in his heart. He has the rest of Matthew 11 verse 28, but not the one of verse 29.

The one in verse 29 is a special kind of rest. It is a rest in the soul, which is a rest in the inward being. Psalm 42.5 asks, "Why art thou cast down, O my soul? And why art thou disquieted within me?" The soul may cause us to be cast down and disquieted. But rest which the Lord will give us is that of the soul, enabling us to live in this world without worry and agitation.

The Lord continued by telling us the reasons for His own rest in the soul. "For I am meek and lowly in heart." The first reason is to be found in the word "meek"; the second reason is to be found in the word "lowly." What is meekness? It is a tenderness without any tinge of hardness. The Lord has nothing in Him which will irritate anybody. He is so tender and delicate that He will not refuse anyone nor think of himself. He is as soft as the touch of water. Such is the kind of life our Lord manifested in the world.

Yet, though many people may manifest meekness towards others, they are not lowly in their hearts. Outwardly they are meek, but in heart they are proud. To be lowly means to take the low position. The Lord is lowly in heart, which means, He considers himself to be deserving of such low treatment because He does not expect anything better. When He one day preached in His home town of Nazareth and was opposed and persecuted by the inhabitants, it was said of Him that He "passing through the midst of them went his way" (Luke 4.30). On earth Jesus was not only meek but He was also lowly. He knew that that was His portion on earth; He did not expect any higher treatment. Pride is in the heart as well as in appearance. If I esteem myself better than other people, if I covet that which God has not given me, if I seek something for myself, then I am proud.

The attitude our Lord continually maintained while on earth was one of meekness and lowliness. For us who are Christians to find that rest of which He spoke, we need to do two things: first, to "take my yoke upon you"; and second, to "learn of me." A yoke is a wooden rod placed upon the back of an ox to keep it from moving freely so that it may work diligently. In the land of Judea, the yoke was always shared by two oxen instead of it being placed on only one ox. The yoke was put on the ox by its master; and hence the Lord our Master says to us to "take His yoke upon us." This yoke is apportioned to us by God and not by man nor by the devil. It is given by God, and it is chosen by us.

Bear the Yoke of Christ

Whatever is appointed by God, and if taken by us, shall make us happy. If I am satisfied, I will have peace. I have nothing to be unhappy about because I have not escaped from the yoke of God appointed to me.

I have a schoolmate who was reared in an orphanage. He was quite bright, and he studied well. He was a church member, yet he was not a born-again Christian. His ambition was to acquire a high degree of education, to attain great fame, and to earn big money. In the year of his graduation from Trinity College in Foochow, a missionary wanted to send him to the United States to study. But as a preparation, he was asked to first go to St. John's University to finish the two years' course which he still lacked. The school would provide a scholarship for him.

However, a few months ago he got saved, and he heard the call of God to preach the gospel. The yoke of the Lord came to him at that time. Yet he inwardly mused how miserable life would be if he became a preacher, especially a country preacher. He would have little income and his living would be rather poor. All his plans and ambition would disintegrate. The expectation of his mother as well as that of his uncle concerning him would come to nought. He did not want to bear the yoke which God gave to him. He thought of escaping. So he promised the principal that he would go to St. John's University.

One day I sought him out and asked him if he had decided on his future. He told me he had decided to go to University to study. I knew, of course, that God had called him. I therefore said to him quite frankly that he had chosen the wrong road, and how, then, could he expect to find rest? "The hope of my elderly mother and of my uncle is upon me," he replied; "I will study literature on the one hand and do research in theology on the other. I will also do some personal work for the Lord in school. Will not this thus accomplish a double purpose?" "To obey is better than sacrifice," I responded. "The Lord takes no pleasure in the cattle on a thousand hills or the sheep on a million hills. He does not delight in fat or burnt offerings, but in hearkening to His voice." "But I have already decided," retorted my friend. "You have nonetheless chosen the wrong way," I replied. "If you go to that university and become contaminated with the poison of the new theology, I am afraid your faith will be overturned and we can no longer walk together in the Way." I then said good-bye to him.

After I left him, my schoolmate walked around the athletic field with a heavy heart. He had no peace within. Later he went to the school chapel, knelt down and prayed. As he thought of his deceased father and widowed mother, as well as of his own future, he wept bitterly. He contemplated deserting the yoke of God, but he had no peace in his heart. Yet how difficult it was for him to obey. Finally, though, he realized he must obey the will of God; so he promised the Lord he would abandon the opportunity for further study and go and preach the gospel instead. After he prayed and obeyed, he got up and found peace and joy in his heart. He immediately sought out his principal and told him the reason for his change of mind. He rejected the offer of a scholarship as well as the help for study abroad promised him by the missionary. He moved out of school. He later testified that that night was the happiest in his life. (Please note that I have no intention of asking anyone not to study. But if God should call you to preach, then you must obey. And if you are *not* called to preach, you may study as long as you wish.)

I know many Christians who have had the same kind of experience just described. You have no rest when you debate with God, asking *Him* to compromise. Your conscience tells you that you are wrong. How miserable you are! But you find rest when you say to God, I will take up the yoke. What God is leading us into today is for us to be willing to take up His yoke in the small things of each day as well as in the big things in life. Some preachers find it hard to labor with their fellow-workers; some sisters find it arduous to live with their in-laws; some employees find it difficult to work with their colleagues; and some students become weary of their relationships with teachers as well as with other students. These are yokes to bear. You are of course tired of them. You wish you could leave them or that they would leave you. You feel cast down and have no peace. Please understand, however, that this is the yoke which God has given you; this is the yoke that He wants you to bear; this is the portion God has appointed to you. He wants you to submit to such a circumstance because it is the best for you.

What is meant by taking up the cross? It is not the spending of thousands of dollars to purchase on the Mount of Olives in Jerusalem a wooden cross to bear. It is for each to bear the yoke in his or her particular situation, for this is God's given portion to you. You consider your environment as bad and wish you could change places with other people, but such would not constitute for you the bearing of a yoke.

Sometimes God puts a careful person and a careless person together, or a strong person and a weak person together, or a healthy person and a sick person together, or a clever person and an ignorant person together, or a quick-tempered person and a slow-tempered person together, or a tidy person and a sloppy person together. So that one will be the yoke to the other, and vice versa. This gives them both the opportunity to learn the nature of Christ. And if you struggle against it, you will have no rest. But if you say to God, "I will take up the yoke You give me, I am willing to take my place, I am willing to obey," you will find rest and joy.

The reason Christians today are weak in bearing a good testimony is because they resist the yoke of God. They want a change in their environment, not realizing that their Christian character is to be made manifest through such environment. The highest life we can live is to welcome all that we naturally dislike. Let me tell you that you will be filled with the deepest rest within if you will joyfully accept the yoke which God gives you. What I speak of here is not the rest of salvation which is given you through the accomplished redemption of Christ on Calvary's cross. This is instead a rest which depends on your obedience, your attitude of self-denying, and your taking up the cross yourself.

I hope all of us will find such a new rest, which, unlike snow that can be quickly shaken off one's overcoat on a wintry day, we do not attempt to shy away from. You and I have no need to struggle over our environment appointed to us, for we can tell

God, "I thank You, because this is Your yoke"; even as our Lord Jesus said: "Yea, Father, for so it was well-pleasing in thy sight." And thus will we have joy. Although what happened to the Lord Jesus was most trying, He did not murmur, nor worry, nor plot. He simply obeyed, and hence He could be joyful. We should obey God for the sake of joy, for in obeying Him we do indeed find joy. I know that all of us have many people around us whom we can neither love nor easily labor together with, but I hope henceforth we all will accept whatever comes from God's hand and take up that meek and lowly yoke.

Learn of the Lord

We must not only take up the yoke but also learn from the Lord. His attitude is recorded in Philippians 2.6–8 which states: "who, existing in the form of God, counted not the being on an equality with God a thing to be grasped, but emptied himself, taking the form of a servant, being made in the likeness of men; and being found in fashion as a man, he humbled himself, becoming obedient even unto death, yea, the death of the cross." Two points need to be emphasized here.

First, the Lord never stands up for His own rights nor speaks for himself; "who, existing in the form of God, counted not the being on an equality with God a thing to be grasped, but emptied himself." Our Lord is equal with God, sharing equally with Him in His glory and power. The Lord Jesus is one with God.

Yet, though it was His right to do so, He did not lift up himself; on the contrary, He emptied himself and took the form of a bondservant, rather than remain equal with God which was His right. How totally unlike the devil who, being a created archangel, desired to raise himself up to be equal with God. Jesus was completely opposite from the devil. Instead of remaining equal with God, He emptied himself. Please remember, therefore, that none of us should speak on behalf of his or her own rights. Every one of us must be willing to forfeit his legitimate rights.

A sister once ruled her house like a queen, then got saved, and became almost like a maid. When she asked her parents for some pocket money and she was not given it as quickly as before, she was willing to lay aside her position and privilege as a daughter. Being now a Christian, you cannot expect your parents to necessarily treat you any more as their child or expect your friends to necessarily deal with you kindly as before. If they refuse to give you your rights, you should put yourself in God's hand and learn concerning the Lord, one "who, existing in the form of God, . . . [nevertheless] emptied himself." He never spoke for himself, therefore we should not speak for ourselves either.

The rest of a Christian lies not only in his not owing anything to anybody but also in enduring whatever he is owed. Many young Christians had defrauded others before they were saved. But afterwards they try to be fair with people. When Christians now experience any unfairness they feel angry. They do not know that believers must not only be fair to others but must also endure any unfairness meted out to them by others. What the Lord received from others was certainly not fairness. In all frankness and fairness, He had no need to come to this world to become a man in order to save us. But for our sake He was willing to endure all unfair treatment.

Second, "taking the form of a servant, being made in the likeness of men." This means He accepted limitation. In heaven, our Lord is free to move wherever He wishes; He could even appear to earthly men as the Angel of God as was often recorded in the Old Testament. But after He was incarnated and took upon himself the likeness of men, He grew up from babyhood to manhood. He grew according to the age of men, and as man He needed to eat and drink as well as to sleep and rest. This was a tremendous restriction to His Deity. Indeed, He became even more limited by taking the form of a bondservant. As a man, He might not have the freedom of God, yet He still had the freedom of men as well as experiencing the enjoyment that men have. Now, though, taking the form of a bondservant, He sacrificed even the freedom of an ordinary man. He was restricted and bound in all His ways; He knew nothing except His Father's will. What restriction He must have accepted in His humanity! Though being the infinite God, the Lord Jesus accepted finite limitation; and though He became man, He accepted even further restriction.

What about us? Oh, how our hearts rebel against any limitation. How we long to break every bondage and restriction that we may move freely. How we hope that the entire world, be it people or things or events, would submit to our will. How unlike Christ we are. Though He is God, yet He accepted limitation. Some mothers dream of not being mothers but preaching the gospel instead—once a sister told me that if her husband would permit it, she would leave her three children and go preach the gospel in Tibet. She yearned to have all bonds cut off that she might fly away. This, however, is not the Lord's attitude. He is God, yet He was obedient to His earthly parents and cared for His brothers and sisters in the flesh. How we too ought to learn to be obedient; we should not entertain any improper ambition for ourselves. We should submit joyfully if God uses family or children to limit us. It is wrong for merchants to think of not trading, for students to hope of not studying, for teachers to expect not to teach, and so forth. We shall find rest if like our Lord we are willing to accept all kinds of limitations without struggle.

To sum up, then, an unbeliever may receive rest and be reconciled to God. And a Christian will find rest in his soul if he is willing to take up the meek and lowly yoke and learn of the limitations of the Lord in not standing up for his own rights. Day by day the Christian accepts the yoke which God has apportioned to him and chooses to live a restricted life for the Lord.

"My yoke is easy, and my burden is light," said Jesus. All who are experienced in Christ will say, Amen. How uneven is the way we choose for ourselves! How troublesome are the things which we do according to our own thoughts! How heartbreaking are the consequences! How difficult for us to advance! But if we are willing to take up the Lord's yoke, and learn of Him, we shall truly see how easy and light are the things which God has given us. His demands as well as the environments He has arranged for us are both easy and light. He will not allow us to go through what we are unable to bear. He knows how to measure to us His burden, and He also knows our struggle. Let us rest in Him. He will not ask something of us which we cannot do. What He apportions to each is what each of us can take. Just as no one would place a heavy iron yoke on a calf three months old, so the Lord will not permit any unbearable circumstances to fall on one who cannot bear it.

Hence whatever befalls us, it has been approved by God as being something He knows we have the strength to bear. God makes no mistakes; therefore, let us not murmur. Even though many of the yokes and burdens He gives us we may not like, let us quietly, humbly, meekly and joyfully accept them all as truly from His hand.

5 Watch and Pray

Finally, be strong in the Lord, and in the strength of his might. Put on the whole armor of God, that ye may be able to stand against the wiles of the devil. For our wrestling is not against flesh and blood, but against the principalities, against the powers, against the world-rulers of this darkness, against the spiritual hosts of wickedness in the heavenly places. Wherefore take up the whole armor of God, that ye may be able to withstand in the evil day, and, having done all, to stand. Stand therefore, having girded your loins with truth, and having put on the breastplate of righteousness, and having shod your feet with the preparation of the gospel of peace; withal taking up the shield of faith, wherewith ye shall be able to quench all the fiery darts of the evil one. And take the helmet of salvation, and the sword of the Spirit, which is the word of God: with all prayer and supplication praying at all seasons in the Spirit, and watching thereunto in all perseverance and supplication for all the saints, and on my behalf, that utterance may

> be given unto me in opening my mouth, to make known with boldness the mystery of the gospel, for which I am an ambassador in chains; that in it I may speak boldly, as I ought to speak. (Eph. 6.10–20)

We are all most familiar with this lengthy passage, and therefore I am not going to expound the entire paragraph but will instead focus only on verse 18, which reads: "with all prayer and supplication praying at all seasons in the Spirit, and watching thereunto in all perseverance and supplication for all the saints." Due to the lack of time, moreover, I will not even explain the first and last phrases of this verse 18. We will concentrate our attention only on the words found in the middle of the verse: "praying at all seasons in the Spirit, and watching thereunto in all perseverance."

The apostle says we should be in the Holy Spirit and should pray at all seasons in the Spirit. Even that is not enough, however, since Paul feels he must add one more thing, which is, watching in all perseverance. Now if I were to say you must be watchful because the Lord is coming soon, you would probably understand. If I were to suggest you need to watch when you are under trial, you would also understand. But here the "watching thereunto in all perseverance" of which Paul speaks may be hard for us to grasp. To what does the word "thereunto" point? It can point to but one thing, which is, that it refers back to the praying and supplication mentioned just before it. The apostle is exhorting us to do one thing—namely, that we be watchful with all perseverance in prayer and supplication. He does not say the Lord is coming soon, nor does he mention any trial. He merely speaks of watching with all perseverance in prayer and supplication.

Many readers do not understand what this means. Let us therefore ask God to give us light that we may know what is meant by watching in prayer and supplication. For if we learn how to watch, we have learned much in prayer. Oh, we must be watchful not only in regard to the Lord's second coming, not only in regard to the danger or trial we may be in, but also in regard to the area of prayer and supplication. Yet what does being watchful mean? It means to have the eyes open, to be vigilant lest anything slip away. The apostle here wishes us to be watchful in prayer and supplication—and not only in trial and affliction—because nothing in a Christian's life is attacked more severely than is prayer. Hence we must learn much in prayer if we would advance spiritually.

First: The Time of Prayer

In a Christian's life, no time is subject to attack more than is the time of prayer. It may easily be conceded that we literally cannot find the time to pray. For this reason, unless we are watchful, we simply will not pray.

How strange it is that you have time to eat, to entertain guests, to visit people, and to do many other things, but you cannot find time to pray. Last night, for instance, you acknowledged that a day had passed without you having really prayed. And hence you decided you would find time the next day to give yourself to pray. But on the next day, at the appointed time of prayer, someone turns up knocking at your front door and someone else is looking for you at the back door. How strange that at other times everything is quiet, but at the time of prayer, many odd things begin to happen. If you want to find time for other things, you have the time. It is only when you attempt to find time to pray that you cannot find it. Many are surprised at such experience.

You must recognize the need to be watchful unto prayer. You need to open your eyes wide and be vigilant. You cannot let prayer go by because you do not have the time. You instead ought to investigate why this is so. Realize, please, that this is all the work of Satan. He is trying to disturb you; he purposely creates these obstacles to keep you from praying.

Let me speak most frankly, that the reason why Christians today do not pray well is because they have never examined this matter and kept a watchful eye not to let the time of prayer pass by. This is why Christians have time for Bible study or other work, but they can find no time for prayer. Just here is where Satan prevails. He knows that if believers do not have the time for prayer, they will not pray; and thus he will not be limited in any way.

We know that each time we are watchful it is because there is some danger ahead. Each time we are on guard it is due to an enemy being around. Without any danger or enemy lurking about we would have no need to be vigilant. In other words, whenever there is any need to watch, there must be an enemy or some kind of danger ahead. We must therefore be watchful over the time of prayer and supplication. We must find time to pray. If we wait until we are at leisure to pray, we will never have the opportunity to do so. All who desire to do intercessory work or to make progress in prayer life must "make" the time by setting aside a period for prayer. Let us guard this period and hold fast to it. Let us beseech God to give us the time to pray. We must pray the prayer of protection for our prayer time. Pray that the period of prayer may not be lost. For with any such loss we will pray no more.

May all who desire to serve God keep well in mind that their prayer time is the period they must themselves set aside. Andrew Murray once said that whoever does not have an appointed time of prayer has no prayer. Without setting aside a special period for prayer, no one will ever have the time to pray. Yet not only this, but even after a person *has* decided on a time, he must use prayer to protect that time. He must surround his time with prayer so that the enemy may not snatch it away. And this is what is thus meant by watching "thereunto." That which the Christian must watch concerns first of all the very time of prayer.

Second: At the Time of Prayer

We must not only watch over the time of prayer but also guard vigilantly how best to use that time. We must not only look for time to pray, we must keep watch over that time as well. How do we explain this? Well, we realize that at no time is a Christian attacked more than at the time he is praying. During ordinary times, your head may be clear and your thought coherent. But during the time of prayer, your thoughts begin to wander and to become confused. You do not know where you are being drawn to. Initially your body is full of strength, but as you start to pray, your body immediately feels tired and drowsy. In other situations you can usually talk with people until eleven or twelve o'clock at night or you are able to work until a very late hour; but when at nine o'clock you try to pray, you sense a drag and want to go to sleep. You do not understand why initially you are well, but at the moment you begin to pray, you feel tired. You wonder why, if you do other things at that time your spirit seems strong, but that you lose your strong spirit in the moment of prayer.

The explanation for this is that the enemy is hindering you from praying. He wants to cut your line of heavenly communication because he knows the power of prayer. He realizes how prayer will restrict him and how it will bring down power from heaven. Accordingly, the enemy tries his best to attack your prayer. He realizes that unless he manages to cut this line of communication he will suffer loss. He reasons that he can do anything to you according to his whim if only he can hinder you from communing with God. As a consequence, you may do other things without any interference from him, but you will incur his inconvenient attacks once you launch into prayer.

How should we deal with this kind of situation?

There is no other way but to be watchful. Hence we must guard the proper *use* of the prayer period as well as the period of prayer itself. Let us open our eyes wide lest we be deceived into thinking we cannot pray today because we do not feel well. We should be aware of the fact that this is but the enemy's attack. Let us not give in to the thought that we cannot pray because we are tired and that we will damage our health if we insist on praying. Such is but the deception of the enemy. If any of us feels weak at the time of prayer, we must not take it as being natural. Furthermore, if we find our thoughts wandering at prayer time, we must not accept this as being natural either. All these simply come from Satan to deceive as well as to attack us.

Therefore, be watchful: "watching thereunto in all perseverance." Use prayer to protect your prayer. Surround your prayer with prayers. Before you do the work of prayer, petition God to enable you to pray without being hindered, that you may pray without feeling weak and sleepy, that you may pray with spirit and concentration, and that you may be protected by the Blood. Tell the Lord: "Lord, protect my prayer that I may concentrate and be powerful in it without being hindered by apparent natural weakness."

Take note that there are two kinds of soldiers on earth: one is the regular soldier who goes to the front to fight, and the other is the sentry. A sentry is not for fighting, he is instead used for self-protection—that is to say, to guard those who are the fighting men. You may have observed a company of soldiers stationed in a compound. Invariably there will be some soldiers with weapons standing at the entrance. Why do these soldiers stand there? To guard the fighting men within lest the latter be attacked. We know that prayer is also fighting and attacking Satan. We need sentry prayer to protect our fighting prayer. To be watchful is to post a sentry. Hence "watching thereunto in all perseverance" means we must carefully set a watch lest the fighting men (that is to say, our prayers) suffer loss.

In short, we need to watch over two things: first, we must not allow Satan to rob us of our prayer time; and second, upon allocating the time, we must ask the Lord to so protect this time that we may have the strength to properly use it for the work of prayer. And never forget that these apparently adverse conditions are not real but false, they merely being the deceit of the enemy.

Third: Prevent All That Is Not Prayer

In order to pray well, there are many things we have to do. Among them is preventing all that is not prayer. For the enemy will not only take away your energy as well as your time to pray, he will additionally induce you to use many empty words. This is also something to which you should have your eyes wide open. You must refuse to waste your prayer time. The prayers of a great number of people are not real; they use many vain words which fail to accomplish any work.

Once I heard of an incident concerning Evan Roberts. At first I could hardly believe it. You may know that Mr. Roberts was the great revivalist in Wales. On one occasion there were a few believers praying in his parlor for a specific matter. When one of the brothers had prayed through half of his prayer, Mr. Roberts went over to him and with his hand stopped his mouth and said, "Brother, do not continue on, because you are not praying." When I read of this, I thought this was impossible, and yet Mr. Roberts had done it. I know now that he was right in so doing.

Many words in our prayer come from our flesh. Our prayer may be long-drawn-out with many words which are not real or effective. Frequently, in our time of prayer we circle around the world several times, using up time and energy without obtaining any answer to real prayer. Though you have prayed much, your prayer will not be answered nor will it be effective. You simply expend your time and strength ill-advisedly. Prayer need not be too long. There is no necessity to insert many speeches into it. Be careful lest you have too much argument in your prayer. We need only to present our heart desire before God. That alone is enough. We should not add many other things to it.

If what you say are empty words, you yourself know that God will not hear you. We must therefore take note and be watchful. What do we need to watch? Watch that we do not say any word carelessly before God. There was once a Christian who was quite powerful in prayer. He at one time wrote a hymn in which was found this sentiment: If you come to God, please prepare beforehand what you will ask.

Let me inquire of you, How would you go to a judge to present your case? Would you go empty-handed? No, you first would prepare a petition. In a similar manner ought we to go to God. You and I must first prepare what we wish to pray. We ought not approach Him without having any idea what we want. Oftentimes prayers have no power and accomplish no work and therefore go unanswered. Such a result can frequently be attributed to the fact that our prayers are aimless because they are accompanied by idle words. This again is the wile of Satan. He gets us to utter idle words which are absolutely useless. Our prayers in such case will return to us without changing anything. For this reason, we must watch with vigilance in our prayer.

You thus must first know what your heart desire is. You need to be clear as to what you will ask of God. You cannot come without some aspiration. If there is no heart desire, there can be no real prayer, for all prayers are governed by heart desire. Once a blind man asked the Lord, "Jesus, thou Son of David, have mercy on me"! The Lord answered him, "What wilt thou that I should do unto thee?" (see Mark 10.46–52). Now the Lord today would also ask of you, "What do you want from Me in your prayer?" Many people may have prayed for fifteen or twenty minutes. If you were to pull them aside and ask them what they had asked of God, they would probably not be able to tell you anything exact. Though they have said much, they do not know what they want. There is no heart desire. How can you expect to be used by God in this work of prayer if there is no preparation of heart? We must pay attention to our heart desire before we ever come to pray. Let us search diligently as to what we really want.

There is another matter of equal importance in prayer. It concerns the phraseology we use in it. You will recall how one day a Syrophoenician woman came to the Lord asking for healing of her daughter. The Lord responded by saying: "It is not meet to take the children's bread and cast it to the dogs." Now the Gentiles were considered by the Jews to be dogs. This woman, though, did not mind being termed as such. If she was looked upon as a dog, then let her be viewed as a dog! So she replied, "Yea, Lord; even the dogs under the table eat of the children's crumbs." Now listen to what the Lord then answered her with: "For this saying go thy way; the demon is gone out of thy daughter" (see Mark 7.24–30). This incident indicates to us how important our phraseology before God is. The Lord answered this woman's request because she has uttered the right phrase. Hence, besides having a proper heart desire before God, we must also see to it that we have the right words with which to express our desire. How often we truly have a heart aspiration within, yet after we pray for a while our words begin to drift away from the burden we have. Let us realize that all powerful prayers have excellent phraseology. Yet this observation is not meant to imply that we should in advance compose a good prayer and then recite it to God.

We have now come to understand two important things concerning prayer: we must pay attention to guard our heart desire and to use the proper words.

We shall next notice a third thing. We need to watch as to how we ask. A most pitiful thing is that many who have a proper desire and the right words do not know how to watch themselves in prayer. So that before long their words have drifted far afield—way beyond the point of return. For this reason, in prayer we need to make sure our words do not run wild. Especially in loud prayers should we carefully examine to see if our words have wandered far from the subject. If so, we must draw them back. Such wandering can easily happen because although at the beginning we really have something in heart to ask, yet as we utter one sentence after another we can unconsciously leave the center and move the words of our prayer into other directions. If we realize we have indeed left the center, we must begin anew and redirect our words back to the subject. Let us be careful in having our prayer "hitched" to the goal we have in mind without any let up. It is important in prayer that it is maintained with vigilance and firmness so that no unnecessary words may filter in. What is being emphasized here is that we not allow any unnecessary or vain words to infiltrate our prayer. We must guard against many speeches and arguments invading our prayers.

In conclusion, then, the points we have just discussed include these three things: first, that in order to eliminate ineffective prayer, we must have a heart desire, that is to say, we must have in view a specific object for which to ask; second, we need to have exact phraseology—our words must be right; and third, we should maintain a good condition during prayer by not allowing unimportant words to be added to our prayer so that we are kept from praying what is not prayer.

Fourth: Praying at All Seasons

For our prayer to be truly effective, we must spread out our prayer like a net. What does this mean? It means we must pray with all prayers so that nothing is left out which should be prayed for. We will not allow anything to slip away. Without such a "prayer net" we will not be able to obtain good results. A person who knows how to pray knows how to pour out his heart desire completely before God. He will use all kinds of prayers to surround as with a net the thing he prays for so that the adversary can do absolutely nothing. Nowadays our prayers are too loose, they are not tight enough. Though we may use many words, our prayers are not well-rounded, thus providing the enemy loopholes through which to make his attack. But if our prayers are like spreading nets, the enemy will have no opening by which to get in. And thus shall our petitions before God be realized.

Let us take the following as an example of this. Suppose a brother situated locally goes to the borderland to preach the gospel. In support of him you have a heart to be responsible for him in prayer. With such an earnest desire, you must lay before God in prayer everything you can think of in connection with this brother's mission to the borderland. You pray for his needs, the train he must take, the rail tracks of the train, his ticket, porters, luggage, lodging on the way, food, health, and the people he will meet on the train. You pray for the house in which he will stay after his arrival, the local people, his manners and attitude among the people he will serve, his preaching, his first work, and his needs for food and clothing in the borderland area. In short, you pray for everything you can think of in relation to this brother. You even pray for the delivery of his mail, asking God to protect every piece that none will be lost or stolen. This is praying with all prayers, by which you spread as it were a net for that brother, leaving nothing unprayed for so that he may have peace in all things. Satan will not be able to do anything towards that brother because you have already surrounded him with a protective net. With such a prayer net, the enemy's hand is completely tied.

Such kind of prayer naturally requires watching, for unless you watch, you will not know that there are so many aspects you need to pray for on his behalf. A hasty prayer or a passing prayer, a prayer overly economized in time, is usually a careless prayer which gives the adversary loopholes by which to enter in. Oftentimes such a careless prayer signifies a shallow desire. If you did have a deep desire, you would be compelled by the burden within you to pray with all prayers. Naturally, this of which we have been speaking has a close relationship to knowledge. You must therefore watch and open your eyes wide so that you may pray for everything you notice and think of. If you do not watch, your prayer may be concluded in two sentences, since you have nothing more to pray about.

Hence to serve the Lord well in prayer, we need to be watchful concerning time, attitude, and all the various aspects of things until all have been prayed for. This is not an easy task, but it is an expression of great love. If there is no love there, will there be such intercession? Without real love no one will intercede; no child of God will do the work of intercession.

Fifth: Watch after Prayer

A good physician will not only be careful in prescribing medicine but will in addition consider the effect on the patient after he has taken it. For the doctor knows that as the patient's symptoms change, his physiology changes too. The physician must therefore change his method of care. In a similar way, with respect to prayer, after you have prayed, you must be watchful for any new discovery, new change or new attitude. You need to observe continuously if any new phenomenon appears in the person or thing that you prayed for. Otherwise, even though you have prayed, it will be of no avail if there is no watchfulness. It is very essential for you to watch "the afterwards" of the person or thing you prayed for. This will affect your prayer before God. Prayer must not only be with all prayers but in all seasons as well. Not just pray once, but pray many times. Not only with all prayers at one time, but with all prayers in all seasons. Without vigilance, prayer frequently becomes powerless. And thus we must be watchful *after* prayer.

Take as another example the following situation. Say that you pray for one who opposes the Lord. You ask God to make him believe. You pray for him with all prayers, and not just once but in all seasons. Meanwhile, you believe in God's promise and lay hold of His word. After several days, the situation appears to grow worse. He opposes the Lord more than ever before. Many people may ignore the phenomenon and keep on praying the old prayers. This is wrong. Prayer alone is not enough. You must observe and lay his opposition before God, telling Him that the man has increased his opposition. At the same time, you ask God why his condition has worsened and what you should now do. If you are watchful, God may give you light and let you know that this is due to the fact that your prayer has already affected the adversary; otherwise there would not be such a change. The enemy is afraid you will snatch this man away, and hence he has stirred up further opposition in the man. So you may begin to praise God. Although the outward opposition is increased, you know your prayer has touched that person. That is why the enemy has to throw a tighter protective ring around him. But you can now change to another kind of prayer and spread a new net. Perhaps after a little time has elapsed, his attitude begins to soften. Formerly he would ignore you, but now he seems willing to talk with you. At this juncture, you need to spread still another prayer net. In other words, you need to alter your prayer according to the changing circumstances. For this, however, it demands much watching. One thing is certain here: that knowledge governs prayer. The clearer you are about a matter, the easier you can pray for it. Hence if anyone asks you to pray for a certain matter that person should clearly tell you about it. For you can pray only as much as you know.

Watching will help us to know which direction our prayer should go as well as how much change has occurred in the person or thing prayed for. We must continually be on the watch so as to notice the effect of our prayer as to whether the situation grows worse or gets better, whether it advances or retreats. Oftentimes we need to keep on watching a person, a work, a trial, or even a brother—because we must be not only faithful but also wise. Our eyes should be as open as they are closed. We need to close our eyes in order to pray faithfully for people, but we need also to open them to notice any change. If we merely close our eyes, the enemy will have plenty of opportunities to deceive us. In Ephesians 6, where spiritual warfare is spoken of, the most important element in it is mentioned last, which is that of prayer. But this prayer needs to be supported with watching. Only in this way will our prayer be effective.

Let us understand that the basic essential is to pray. But if we wish our prayer to be powerful, we must add to it the matter of watching. Unfortunately, many people today have not learned how to do the work of prayer. They are rather vague about it. Today we have no other motive than expecting God to revive us into doing this work. Please do not forget that in the life of every child of God the most attacked facet of his walk is prayer. For without prayer, there will be no power. Because of this fact, Satan especially tries to disturb the Christian's prayer life—causing him to have neither time nor strength to pray, causing him to use many vain words in his prayer, to omit many things without the matter being properly covered in prayer, and to fail to observe the changes after prayer.

In order to learn well how to pray, a person needs to pay attention to these five points. Although these matters are seemingly rather simple, they are nonetheless quite profound. People who have prayed for years have learned these five things well; beginners in prayer, on the other hand, should attend diligently to these five points. And as time goes on, they shall become more experienced in prayer.

May God be gracious to us today that we may pay attention to these five points.

6 The Other Aspect of the Trespass-Offering

Jehovah spake unto Moses, saying, If any one sin, and commit a trespass against Jehovah, and deal falsely with his neighbor in a matter of deposit, or of bargain, or of robbery, or have oppressed his neighbor, or have found that which was lost, and deal falsely therein, and swear to a lie; in any of all these things that a man doeth, sinning therein; then it shall be, if he hath sinned, and is guilty, that he shall restore that which he took by robbery, or the thing which he hath gotten by oppression, or the deposit which was committed to him, or the lost thing which he found, or any thing about which he hath sworn falsely; he shall even restore it in full, and shall add the fifth part more thereto: unto him to whom it appertaineth shall he give it, in the day of his being found guilty. And he shall bring his trespass-offering unto Jehovah, a ram without blemish out of the flock, according to thy estimation, for a trespass-offering, unto the priest. (Lev. 6.1–6)

Let us study very carefully this portion of the Scriptures. It speaks of the trespass-offering which is a very important matter in the Bible. From Leviticus chapter 1 through chapter 6, five different offerings are mentioned. These five typify the different aspects of our Lord offering himself up as a sacrifice. Our Lord Jesus Christ is the sacrifice of God which can be viewed from five different perspectives. Only by so viewing it can the presentation of the sacrifice be complete.

The Relationship of the Trespass-Offering to the Other Four Offerings

What is the relationship between the trespass-offering and the four offerings previously mentioned? In order to answer this, we need to describe these four briefly before we can make a comparison with the trespass-offering.

1. *Burnt-offering.* This one signifies how our Lord offers himself up wholly to God. It is not for atonement, but by offering himself voluntarily to God He makes the work of atonement possible.

2. *Meal-offering.* There is no blood in this offering, because this one typifies the life of our Lord. His life on earth is most pure—He having lived purely and delicately before God. The emphasis of this offering is on His perfection. He is the perfect Man. Just as flour is good to men, so to us who believe He is our spiritual food.

3. *Peace-offering.* This one symbolizes the Lord making peace between God and men. He causes us to

be at peace with God as well as causes God to be at peace with us.

4. *Sin-offering.* This offering suggests how through His redemptive work the Lord reconciles us to God. He makes atonement for our sins that we may be saved by His work.

5. *Trespass-offering.* Some may ask what is the difference between the sin-offering and the trespass-offering? "Sin" points to the sum total of our transgressions before God, whereas "trespass" refers to the sins we commit daily, we therefore being accountable. It may be said that the sin-offering is for our *total* sin, while the trespass-offering is offered up for our various particular sins which may be counted.

The Two Aspects of the Trespass-Offering

The trespass-offering contains two parts: the first is recorded in Leviticus 5 and the second, in Leviticus 6. In chapter 5 we are told what we must do before God for the daily sin we commit against Him. Chapter 6 shows us what we must do to men if we have sinned against them in our daily life. What we shall focus on now is not chapter 5 but chapter 6, which deals with the action we need to take if we sin against men after we are saved.

The Importance of the Trespass-Offering

I am not to be understood as saying that this offering may save us. We already have the burnt-offering, meal-offering, peace-offering and sin-offering—which all save us and give us life. The trespass-offering of chapters 5 and 6, however, deal with the problem of communion with God. To have life is one thing, to commune with God is another. As you believe in the substitutionary death of Christ and receive Him as your Savior, you have eternal life. But this does not imply that hereafter you will never once lack communion with God. It is true you are saved and that you have communion with God. Yet days after you are saved, you may lose communion with Him if you again sin and refuse to repent. At that time you feel you are far away from God, and you find it hard to pray and to read the Bible. This is not to suggest you are no longer saved. Since you believe, you are saved; and this will never change. Nevertheless, your communion with God is often changeable. If you should not get rid of your sin, you will lose communion with God. Many are saved, but they find prayer and Bible reading a great difficulty. This may be due to their failure to deal with their daily sins.

As soon as we are saved, we have the joy of salvation. We are eager to tell everybody how happy we are that we are saved. Unfortunately, such joy does not last long. Why do we lose it? Perhaps we have spoken an unkind word and have sinned against somebody. And hence we feel ashamed to approach God. The one we have sinned against is another person, yet the one who loses joy is ourselves. We sin against men, but we lose communion with God.

Today we want to learn the lesson of not only being saved but of also maintaining a living communion with God daily as well as to have good prayer, good Bible reading, and a good testimony every day. We can lose communion, though we will never lose salvation: "They shall never perish, and no one shall snatch them out of my hand. My Father, who hath given them unto me, is greater than all; and no one is able to snatch them out of the Father's hand" (John 10.28b,29). So says the Lord. Eternal life can never be lost, but there is one thing which may be lost—probably many times a day—and that is our communion with God.

Suppose, for example, a father has told his son he must behave and not do certain things. The son then steals a piece of candy in the cupboard, or plays with bad company, or soils his clothes with dirt. When he hears his father calling him, the son dare not face him. They still have the relationship of father and son; nevertheless, due to his doing something which his father will not be pleased with, the son dare not see the father's face immediately. His heart beats fast as he hears his father's voice, for he knows something is wrong between the two of them. He thinks to himself, How can I face my father? Will this change his relationship as son to his father? Certainly not. *That* relationship will never change; but the *fellowship* between them *will* change. In like manner, let us see that our relationship with God as our Father and we as His children is a life relationship which is not subject to change according to the changing condition of our daily life. What *does* change is that we lose our daily communion with God.

The trespass-offering leads us back to the restoration of our communion with God. As the sin-offering brings sinners to believe in the Lord Jesus, so the trespass-offering leads Christians back to communion with God. The sin-offering takes away our sins which occurred in the days we were yet unbelievers; the trespass-offering, though, gets rid of that which hinders our daily communication with God. One gives us life; the other gives us communion.

The Aspect of the Trespass-Offering towards Men

We have already mentioned how the trespass-offering has two aspects: Leviticus chapter 5 shows us what we must do if we sin against God, whereas chapter 6 shows us what we must do if we sin against men. The latter aspect is what we would talk about here. If we have sinned against men, thus causing us to have our communion with God interrupted, what must we do? Simply remember that chapter 6 does not deal with salvation unto life but with how to restore our communion with God.

Some Trespasses against Men

"Jehovah spake unto Moses, saying" (6.1). This indicates that what follows is given by God, not by Moses. God tells us what the things are by which we may trespass against other people. It would appear as though God were giving us a list here.

"If any one sin, and commit a trespass against Jehovah" (v.2). If the trespasses listed below are against men, why do we have here the words "commit a trespass against Jehovah"? Simply because whatever trespasses are against men are also trespasses against God. God is the Creator who created mankind, and hence any sin committed against men constitutes a sin against God.

1. *Being unfaithful in trust:* "Deal falsely with his neighbor in a matter of deposit" (v.2). Such sin will most certainly interrupt our communion with God. Has anyone ever entrusted you with something? Once when I returned to Foochow, someone asked me to take some mangoes to my second aunt. Being a kind of tropical fruit, mango is easily spoiled. Though I tried greatly to keep them from spoiling, their color turned somewhat and they were near the point of spoilage. I thought to myself, If I bring them home, they shall probably spoil; so why not give some of them away for the other passengers on the steamer to eat? I therefore chose three green ones to keep, and gave the rest to the passengers on board. As I was approaching home, however, I felt somewhat uneasy because I was not being faithful to my neighbor's trust, since these mangoes did not belong to me. Whether they were still green or spoiled, I should deliver them all to my second aunt. I felt embarrassed about explaining to my relative, yet *not* to explain was equally hard, for this would amount to unrighteousness. Finally, I did explain to my aunt what had happened on the steamer.

If people were to entrust us with fifty dollars, we would probably be faithful. But if we were to be entrusted with fifty pennies, we would perhaps not be so honest; because the amount is small, we will not consider them important. Nonetheless, such conduct would be dealing falsely with people, and it would cause us to lose our communion with God. If we are asked to carry a letter, we may not actually open it and read the contents, yet we may wish to examine the outside of it. Now to glance at it unintentionally would not matter, but it would be wrong if we wished to probe the secrets of others. Such can hinder our living and having intimate fellowship with God. I am afraid many do not study the Bible well because of such sin not being dealt with. If we are unfaithful and do not deal with it, we may lose that freedom of communion with God which is so vital to maintain.

2. *Dealing falsely in bargain:* "Deal falsely . . . in a matter . . . of bargain" (v.2). What was mentioned above is a rather common occurrence; but this now before us is not common but is rather special: it is a false dealing in trade. Yet please understand that this is not just a matter for the merchants; even people who are not in business may commit this sin. This is a matter of concern for every brother or sister in Christ.

I heard once about a family of four who were together in a bus. The mother asked her son to count out seventy pennies to be given to the conductor later. Actually she should have paid seventy-two pennies, but she attempted to save back two of them. This was not the dishonesty of the conductor but that of the passenger. Sometimes in a trolley car, three stations may have already been passed before the conductor comes to receive the fare. Will you be honest and pay the full fare? Or will you only pay the necessary amount from the current station? You may think, Why not save the money for myself instead of letting the conductor pocket the money. Yet that is an unrighteous attitude. As a Christian, you should not deal falsely. We Christians should not be careless in these matters. Sometimes in buying things we may inadvertently be given back two dimes. And if we become happy over the extra money gained, it is an indication that we love sin. You may think this to be a small thing, but we as believers cannot let it slip by.

Some brother has remarked to me that without telling a lie no business can ever be carried on. But let me tell you, we must do business honestly. At the beginning this principle may be more difficult to follow, yet at the end it will be profitable. Many honest brethren can testify to this. We do not *need* to lie, nor *should* we lie. If we lie in trade and bargaining, we shall lose our communion with God. This is something we do need to deal with.

3. *Robbing other people:* "In a matter . . . of robbery" (v.2). To rob or to usurp is a committing of the same sin. Whether something not yours is obtained by force or through an improper method is robbery. For example, suppose you are made the executor of a will. Do you faithfully carry out the will or do you try to retain something for your own self? If you alter the will of the deceased through any mishandling of it to suit your preference, you rob other people of their rightful property. Some of you may have been

soldiers or custom inspectors in the past. Whatever you gained by an improper method can be deemed as robbery.

Believe in the Lord and receive life—this is a spiritual fact. Every one who trusts in the blood of the Lamb has his sins forgiven—this is also a spiritual fact. But if you sin against another person, God cannot forgive you on behalf of the other man. Suppose, for example, that I sin against brother Wong. God cannot forgive me on behalf of brother Wong if I only confess my sin to God. Sin committed against other men must truly be dealt with, for although such sin will not take away life, it certainly can interrupt fellowship with God.

4. *Oppressing a neighbor:* "Or have oppressed his neighbor" (v.2). The term "neighbor" in the Old Testament points to another person. It does not necessarily only mean one's next door neighbor. It is a Hebraism. For a mother-in-law to oppress her daughter-in-law, for parents to oppress their children, for teachers to oppress their students, for people in high position to oppress those in low position—any of these is counted as "oppressing one's neighbor" and is an act with which God is not pleased. None of us may live carelessly. We must deal with these things. Many husbands are rather neutral; many wives are ferocious; many mothers are merciless. How frequently we oppress people and ill-treat our servants. Yet they all are equally created by God, and therefore we must not treat them unkindly. Sometimes they are

in the wrong and may be unreasonable, but they do not have the environment, position and education we have. How can we expect them to be as understandable as we are. Even if they are wrong, we cannot oppress them. A Christian should not be unjust to other people, and neither can he oppress anyone. For God is not pleased with either kind of action.

5. *Dealing falsely with lost things:* "Or have found that which was lost, and deal falsely therein" (v.3). Though we may not take this matter seriously, it is nonetheless a trespass. We may speculate that there is nothing unrighteous in picking up what was lost. Still God declares that it is a false dealing. No Christian should take as his own what belongs to other people. Many have the idea that it is better for money to fall into their own pockets than into the pockets of other people. But this is unrighteous thinking. Once on a trolley car I saw someone drop a penny when he was counting out money for the fare. Another person immediately stepped on the coin so that the owner would not be able to find it.

We should not pick up anything and consider it ours, even if it is a handkerchief, a hat, a fountain pen or a letter. For this is unrighteous. We may have done such a thing in the past, but let us try our best to return it. We should either let the one who lost it regain it or deliver the lost item to the local authorities. Otherwise, we have sinned.

6. *Swearing to a lie:* "And swear to a lie" (v.3).

The lie here has a special relationship to what was mentioned just before. If you pick up an item belonging to other people, you are lying if, when you are asked, you say with an oath that you have not taken it. This is not right, and is roundly condemned by God. We should never lie as a means of escaping difficulty.

To lie, commonly speaking, is a way used to escape from being caught. There are three main reasons for lying: (1) because of pride. Lying is used to protect a person's pride. If he has done something wrong, he will lie, when asked about it, if he says he has not done it but somebody else has. Such lying is to save his face. (2) because of being subjected to too demanding a discipline. A too demanding a mother will produce lying children; a too stern a teacher will have lying students; a too exacting a master will result in his having a lying servant. If we are too demanding of people, this will usually cause them to lie. If you are somewhat more lenient, you will be told by people when they have done wrong. But if you will not forgive the slightest mistake, people will tend to lie to you in order to avoid trouble. (3) because of a desire for gain. If by lying you can gain a hundred dollars, why not tell a lie? Lying may gain something for yourself. Some people lie for the sake of pride; some people lie because they are under circumstances that are too demanding; and some people do so for gain. Lying is condemned by God; and lying for gain is doubly condemned.

If you are a nurse, for example, and you intend to

take home some cotton and medicine from the hospital and say when asked by the clerk of the storeroom that these are for patients elsewhere, you are using a lie to make some gain. How easy it is to tell a lie to gain access to public property. But being a Christian, I must not do so. I will only not feel guilty if someone in authority either gives such property to me or allows me to take it.

How to Deal with Such Trespasses

If we have committed such trespasses, what must we do? We know, of course, that they do indeed need to be dealt with.

"Then it shall be, if he hath sinned, and is guilty . . ." (v.4). To sin is an act, to be guilty is to have a case against oneself before God. What should we do when there is a case before God against us?—"He shall restore that which he took by robbery, or the thing which he hath gotten by oppression, or the deposit which was committed to him, or the lost thing which he found, or any thing about which he hath sworn falsely; he shall even restore it in full, and shall add the fifth part more thereto: unto him to whom it appertaineth shall he give it, in the day of his being found guilty" (vv.4,5). This is a very important command. First, restore the thing taken in full to the original owner. Whatever is not yours should not remain in your house. How can you expect the society around you to be clean if you as a Christian are not clean? How can you expect other people to return things taken if you as a Christian do not return them? Every Christian must be clean. We should restore or apologize as much as we can.

There is a basic difference between the nature of the sin-offering and that of the trespass-offering. The sin-offering is "to propitiate" whereas the trespass-offering is "to restore." We are not able to restore *to God* concerning that about which we have sinned against Him, nor can we propitiate men if we sin against them. Our sin must be propitiated before God through the blood of His Lamb. Whatever we sin against men, however, needs to be restored and not to be propitiated. If we are unfaithful in a matter of deposit or if we make gain through improper means, we must restore it to man. If we do not make restoration, we cannot offer a trespass-offering. To be forgiven by God through the blood of the Lord Jesus is truth. But you will lose the communion with God if you, having sinned against men, refuse to make restoration. Whenever you think of what you did, your conscience will be restive. You are therefore not free to commune with God.

Once F. B. Meyer was invited to speak at the Keswick Convention in England. What was the first message he gave at that time? He said this: "One thing we must clear up if we expect God to bless and revive us. And that is, if there is some account you have yet to settle, you must not expect to receive blessing or to be revived." This word was most effective. For the next day all the money orders at the post office in Keswick were sold out. From this incident we may conclude how many Christians are unrighteous.

Many will say, We have not killed anybody nor have we set fire on any house! But let me tell you that if you owe anything to anyone, it may cause you to lose your communion with God. The blood of Christ washes our sins away because it cleanses our conscience. It does not, however, cleanse our heart. Only when our earthly relationships are all cleared up shall our heart be cleansed.

A more difficult situation exists when the head of a household establishes his house on an unrighteous foundation. And if this unrighteousness is not dealt with, good communion with God is almost impossible. For this will press upon his conscience and hinder his growth. Therefore as much as is within your ability, return whatever belongs to others. And if restoration is absolutely impossible, because of the peculiar circumstances involved, the Lord will accept your willing heart. For instance, a certain brother owed tens of thousands of dollars. He had gained a great deal of money through improper means but then he squandered it almost entirely away, for only a few thousand dollars were left to him. Yet he had children to support. He asked me what he should do. I told him, If you had fifty thousand dollars in the bank, would you refuse to return the money owed? If so, then it would not be due to any lack of money on his part but it would be because of his unwillingness to return the money. And if that were the case, God would not let him go free. This brother's conscience, from then on, would not give him any peace. So I advised him to return whatever he had. It was far better, I told him, to be poor than to have a wicked conscience. As long as our sins are left undealt with, our spiritual energy will be drained to exhaustion.

Add the Fifth Part More

"He shall even restore it in full, and shall add the fifth part more thereto" (v.5). Suppose you owe five dollars; then you should return *six* dollars. The extra dollar is the interest. Any trespass against other people and anything gained through improper means should be restored in full and have added to it a fifth part. This is in order to recompense the damage caused to others by our illicit activity. It also means that it is good for us to add more in restoration. In restoring anything, do not return exactly the amount. It is always better to restore a little beyond the exact requirement lest we harm anybody. This is a most important principle. For instance, suppose I quarreled with brother Wong. I then apologized to him later. If I were to say to brother Wong—"I should not have quarreled with you today; I did not behave like a Christian; but neither should you have quarreled with me"—that would be wrong. I indeed have acknowledged my fault, but I only restored in full without adding on the fifth part. If we still mention the other party's fault, it shows we still harbor an unforgiving heart. So when we apologize, it is much better to do somewhat more. We should have the attitude of not only restoring in full but adding the fifth part on as well. This is a very wholesome principle. We need to enlarge the margin. We ought to confess our sin only and not take a swipe at the other person too. Let us restore the extra fifth part as God has ordained. Let the margin be extended.

The Time to Restore

"Unto him to whom it appertaineth shall he give it, in the day of his being found guilty" (v.5). This tells us that *in the very day* of our being found guilty, we need to make restoration. There is no need to wait. As soon as we know, we should restore. We have no need to wait for the moving of the Holy Spirit, since it is obvious that the Holy Spirit has already moved to make us realize our sin. Do not wait, restore today. Do not delay, because that may result in two ill-effects. First, the voice of the conscience may grow dimmer. Whenever the conscience speaks, it is most precious. But how terrible if it ceases speaking. Second, the accusation of the conscience may become so strong that your mouth is sealed from witnessing and you also are given no peace.

Hence, if we trespass against anybody, let us clear it up with that person immediately. Whatever we owe others or whatever things we obtained through improper means ought to be restored to the original owners. Do not be deceived by the thought that if we trespass against men, we need only confess to God and not confess to men. This cannot be. God will forgive you because of the blood of our Lord, but He will not forgive you for other men. Let the restoration be done on the same day it is discovered. Any delay will take away the strength to do it. Restoration requires strength, and the day of discovery is the greatest there will be.

Bring in the Trespass-Offering

"He shall bring his trespass-offering unto Jehovah, a ram without blemish out of the flock, according to thy estimation, for a trespass-offering, unto the priest" (v.6). This is the second thing to do. After you have restored the thing you owe another, there is one more thing you must do. Though you have made restoration to men, you will not have received forgiveness from God. You must offer a trespass-offering to Him. *No one in the world can receive God's forgiveness by confession alone.* If anyone sins against God, he will receive forgiveness through the blood of the Lord. But if he sins against man, he shall first clear it up with man, and then say to God, "O God, I know I have sinned against man, but I have already cleared it up with him. Now, though, I ask You to forgive my sin through the blood of the Lord Jesus." Since you have settled your trespass with man and you now confess your sin to God, your sin will be forgiven by Him through the blood of the Lord Jesus.

"The priest shall make atonement for him before Jehovah; and he shall be forgiven concerning whatsoever he doeth so as to be guilty thereby" (v.7). There is no sin in the world too big for God to forgive. The issue lies in whether or not we confess, because the blood of the Lord Jesus is able to give us forgiveness and to restore to us our communion with Goa

Let us see clearly the place of confession in God's word. Some advocate forgiveness without any confession of sin. That is not adequate. Others champion forgiveness by confession of sin. This is too much. According to the Bible, if anyone sins against man, he should clear it up with man on the one hand and confess to God on the other; and then God will forgive him through the blood of the Lord Jesus. Confessing to God only without also clearing up the matter with man fails to give the conscience peace nor to give the person strength to believe in the power of the blood of the Lord Jesus. Without the blood of the Lord, sin cannot be forgiven: yet without confession to man, the blood of the Lord will not be available for forgiveness either.

Our hope today is to deal with everything in which we have sinned against men so that we may not lose our communion with God.

7 Blessed Are the Meek*

Moses was instructed in all the wisdom of the Egyptians; and he was mighty in his words and works. (Acts 7.22)

The child grew, and she brought him unto Pharaoh's daughter, and he became her son. And she called his name Moses, and said, Because I drew him out of the water. (Ex. 2.10)

It came to pass on the way at the lodging-place, that Jehovah met him, and sought to kill him. (Ex. 4.24)

As we focus our attention on the difference between the wisdom of God and the wisdom of man, we shall see how God judges and rejects the wisdom of man both in life and in work so as to make us acceptable in His sight.

---

*This Chapter constitutes notes that were taken of the October Conference held in 1931 at which the author spoke.—*Translator*

Before we can proceed on this subject, however, we first need to know the three aspects of our flesh which resist God most. These must be dealt with before we can do the good work of God. What are they? First, there is the wisdom of the flesh; second, the strength of the flesh; and third, the vainglory of the flesh. If these have not been crucified, we will not be able to do any good work. For they stand in the most adverse relationship to the work of God. Indeed, they destroy God's work. And their order is always first wisdom, then strength, and finally vainglory. This is their natural order and they are closely linked to one another.

1. God's Operational Tactic: Dealing First with the Man

Moses was the first servant chosen by God. He was the first person called by God to service. Though Abraham, Isaac and Jacob lived before the time of Moses, they were not, strictly speaking, God's servants. They were not covenanted with God as such. Just as Paul may be considered the first servant chosen by God in New Testament times, so Moses may be reckoned as His first chosen servant in the Old Testament period. How did God deal with Moses? In what way did Moses please Him? Before He could deal with the children of Israel, God had first to deal with Moses. Before He could deal with Pharaoh and the Egyptians, He had to deal with Moses.

A servant of the Lord once wrote: When man thinks of doing something he always thinks of the *way* of doing it; but when God intends to do a thing, He usually tries first of all to find the man. Except He finds the right person, God has no way. Today in the church we have all kinds of ways, places, and organizations available, but do we have men? For God does not lay stress on the way, but the man. How very different is man's idea from God's. People assume that a good method will lead to a satisfactory result. Yet they fail to consider the person who executes the method; consequently, they are not able to obtain the good fruit they expect.

The issue, of course, is not that God cannot find people with great talents today; what He cannot find are people who are usable. Three months after he was born, Moses was placed in the water. He was later pulled out of the water by the daughter of Pharaoh who adopted him as her son. Hence the name was given to him of "Moses"—which means "the drawing out of water." He was the first one drawn out. Later on the multitudes of the children of Israel would follow in his train by being drawn out themselves (the Red Sea experience). In the wilderness God dealt with Moses first, and then in the same wilderness He dealt with the children of Israel after they had been led out of Egypt by Moses. Unless *we* are delivered, we cannot expect *other* people to be delivered. If *we* do not have vision, how can we expect *others* to see God's way? Except *we* walk in it, no one *else* will be able to follow. Today God wishes to deal with us first. And after He has gotten some of us, we can then expect to gain other people.

At the beginning of the age of grace God apprehended a few people through whom He was able to cover the entire Roman world with the gospel within three decades. Many new assemblies were raised up. He laid hold especially of Paul, who preached the gospel to the ends of the Roman world. Many believed in the gospel. If we were today like Paul was in the first century, the gospel would already have been preached to all nations. We would have no need today to resort to various means of boosting, propagating, or collecting money in order to draw people to the truth. If only we as persons would be gained by God, all would be well. Can He use you? Does the result of your labor come from your being used by Him or from your using certain means?

To deliver the children of Israel, God must first lay hold of Moses. Without him, God could not save the Israelites. If He did not obtain a man, He did not have any method. If the first man had not been drawn out, the many later would not have been drawn out. If the first man had not been dealt with in the wilderness the many would not have gone to the wilderness later to be dealt with. Except God saved Moses first, He could not have saved the nation of Israel. Now the same principle holds true for us today. Unless God is able to use you, He has no way. If the Holy Spirit has no opportunity to fill you, He cannot work through you to bring salvation to others. You will simply have no power to work, because His power and life have no way to flow out. Only through you can His riches be manifested. In order to be a person whom God can use, you must do two things: trust and obey.

God had made a covenant with Abraham, Isaac

and Jacob to deliver their descendants. He saw how the children of Israel were ill-treated by the Egyptians, and He heard their cry. So He intended to save them according to the covenant He had covenanted with them. But please realize that in order for God to save the people, He must first find a channel, that which could act as a liaison between Him and the people He would save. He must first obtain this channel and then He can work. Moses was that channel whom God used, and he did not fail Him. God was able to use him mightily. Today how many believers have disappointed the Lord because He cannot use them. God is currently looking everywhere to find the man whom He needs and whom He can use.

2. *God Needs the Man Who Knows the Cross*

The qualification for doing God's work does not lie in seminary study, sound faith, zeal, and the love of souls; it instead rests on a person's being totally apprehended by God. He needs men and women who have themselves been crucified so as to preach to others the cross of His Son.

Paul declared: "I determined not to know anything among you, save Jesus Christ, and him crucified" (1 Cor. 2.2). He knew only this and nothing else. He preached only this and nothing else. Let us not wrongly infer that what Paul emphasized was preaching. What he really stressed was knowing. Whether he was at home or abroad, whether he was alone by himself or with other people, whether persuading individuals or preaching publicly, he "knew" the cross just the same. For his entire life was spent under its shadow. God in our day needs people who know the cross far more than He needs those who preach the cross.

When Paul was working among the Corinthians, he said he knew nothing but Jesus Christ and Him crucified. This is how *he* preached the cross: "And I, brethren, when I came unto you, came not with excellency of speech or of wisdom, proclaiming to you the testimony of God. For I determined not to know anything among you, save Jesus Christ, and him crucified. And I was with you in weakness, and in fear, and in much trembling. And my speech and my preaching were not in persuasive words of wisdom, but in demonstration of the Spirit and of power: that your faith should not stand in the wisdom of men, but in the power of God" (1 Cor. 2.1–5).

Please keep in mind that unless you work in the power of God, what you do shall all be in vain. Paul did not use persuasive words of wisdom; rather, he used the power of God in preaching the gospel. His attitude towards himself was one of considering himself as being in weakness, in fear and in much trembling. God must get you to forsake your own wisdom, cleverness and ability before He can use you. What He is looking for today are people who have no confidence in themselves nor are self-reliant and self-willed. If He can find such people, He will use them. He will use them according to the measure of their not trusting in themselves. Yet many people think that so long as their faith is orthodox and they understand the Bible, they can serve God. But I wish to declare that the Holy Spirit can only work through those who are wholly in God's hand. Only people such as this can be channels for the outflowing of the power of life.

Just as Moses was first dealt with by God, you and I must also be dealt with by Him. If God had not dealt with His servant, He could have had no way of dealing with the children of Israel. If He had not dealt with Moses, He could not have dealt with Pharaoh and the Egyptians. And unless He first can deal with us, He has no way to deal with the people of the world as well as the evil spirits. Have we truly been apprehended by God? If so, He will be able to deal with Satan and with the worldly people.

"And being in readiness to avenge all disobedience, when your obedience shall be made full" (2 Cor. 10.6). Paul had to speak to the Corinthian believers in this fashion because he knew very well that he could not deal with those who were in rebellion against God if the majority of the believers there were not themselves first dealt with. He must wait until they obeyed, and only then could he deal with the rebellious. Unless the believers were first dealt with, he had no way to deal with the few remaining ones.

3. God Deals with Moses

From Acts 7.22 we can understand the education which Moses in his earlier years had received: "Moses was instructed in all the wisdom of the Egyptians; and he was mighty in his words and works." He learned all the wisdom of Egypt. He became eloquent and most capable. Yet his learning and ability, his brightness in words and deeds, did not qualify him to be usable by God; on the contrary, these accomplishments became the very reasons why God could *not* use him.

Oh how men look for wisdom and power, but God seeks out the foolish and the weak. 1 Corinthians speaks of the wisdom and power of Christ; it also declares that God chooses the foolish and the weak. The Greeks look for wisdom and the Jews seek for miracles which demonstrate power. But God sets aside man's wisdom and power. For where there is human wisdom, there is also fleshly power. Human wisdom and power can only be effective in human affairs. If they are used in God's work they will destroy it.

God will only use the might and power of the Holy Spirit to accomplish His work. And this might and power is manifested through the foolish and the weak. Unless we are brought by God to forsake in a practical way our own wisdom and power and become as the foolish and the weak before Him, we cannot be used by Him.

How God Deals with Moses' Fleshly Wisdom and Power

We all are familiar with the story of Moses. He had eloquence, wisdom, power and learning. He felt he could do something with these endowments. He saw an enemy oppressing his brethren, so he killed an

Egyptian with his own physical prowess. Then on the next day he found two Israelites striving together. He tried to reconcile them, he no doubt thinking this would be an easy job. To his surprise, he was rejected by them. They even mentioned his killing of the Egyptian the day before. In fear Moses fled to the land of Midian.

What did all this mean? Moses knew only his wisdom and power; he had yet to recognize his foolishness and weakness. God wanted to show him that in relying on himself there were things which he could not do. He sincerely wished to help God in saving the children of Israel, but God had no need of any human help. People who try to help Him with their fleshly wisdom and power will never receive His approval. Many are rejected by Him not because they lack in wisdom and power, but because they are *too* wise and powerful. Hence God cannot use them. He has to set them aside and let them cool down. He will wait until their natural fire is extinguished before He will use them.

Moses was a person who attempted to help God with human wisdom and power. God brought him to a halt and refused to use him since soulish and sentimental wisdom easily stirs up fleshly power. These have absolutely no place in the work of God. During those forty-odd years in the wilderness Moses was not only tried by God, but also taught by Him. He was taught to see how utterly vain everything was that he possessed. Not until then would he be useful.

Yet it is the same with us as well. Nowadays God puts us too in the wilderness, to test us and to teach us. When He sets you aside, you may not understand His will. So that once and again you become rebellious. Again and again He places you there, without giving you favorable enyironment, so that you may submit yourself under His mighty hand. This is to test whether or not you will do His will, for your own will must be dealt with. This is a crisis you must face. The rejection of Moses by the children of Israel was of God. The seeking for his life by Pharaoh was also of God. His flight to the lonely wilderness was likewise of God. After having had numerous communications with God in the wilderness for forty years, he was finally taught by God, he at last realizing his total uselessness. He then no longer dreamed of saving the Israelites with his own ability. He no more thought of himself as a great and mighty man. He ceased to consider himself as being par excellence in the spiritual realm. He at last knew what he could not do. And that was precisely the place which God had wanted him to arrive at all along.

Reckoned Himself As Powerless

Later at Mount Horeb God sent Moses to deliver the children of Israel. Had this happened forty years before, Moses would no doubt have jumped at the chance. But even *without* the command of the Lord, he would have volunteered to go. At that time he only knew what he *could* do; he did not know what he could *not* do. But now Moses was different. He today knew truly what kind of person he was. He also realized finally what his own wisdom and power could not do. So that he told the Lord: "Who am I, that I should go unto Pharaoh, and that I should bring forth the children of Israel out of Egypt?" (Ex. 3.11) How different he now was from what he had been before. Formerly he had conceived the idea he was the only one in the world; now, however, he confessed, "Who am I?" He was no longer self-confident and self-conceited. He looked upon himself as a nobody. And God will bring us to this point as well. This is a spiritual retreat, a holy retreat, a blessed retreat. Unless we see in our heart that we are nothing, we are not yet a person whom God can use.

Moses here confessed how he himself could never bring the children of Israel out of Egypt. He here considered himself to be insignificant and powerless. He recognized at last his own inability. Anyone who has not reckoned himself as such is not fit to work for God. Moses realized now that the work was too great. He also saw his own littleness. He had learned the lesson. He no longer dared to use his natural wisdom and fleshly power. He acknowledged his weakness and disability. He would not even measure himself in the slightest, for he asked God, "Who am I?"—and let God do the measuring for him. He had to be brought to such a point for God ever to use him.

Acknowledged His Lack of Eloquence

But now God had to encourage Moses. All his former boldness, wisdom and power had died; and today all of them must be received anew from God's hand. Such is resurrection. This long period of forty years was like Aaron's staff having to spend the night before the Ark of the Lord. After the night is spent, however, all that has died shall be resurrected.

In God's work, everything must go through death and be resurrected before it can be used. When we observe a young man displaying knowledge, imagination and ability, we most likely will say that that person could be really useful in God's hand were he saved. But allow me to say that though he possesses knowledge, boldness and talent, he is nothing in the hand of God. For the Lord has no use for our wisdom just as He has no use for our foolishness. The wise one should let his wisdom die, even as the foolish one must put his folly to death. Only what emerges in the realm of resurrection can be used by God. Everything belonging to the natural must die, and then shall we receive from God the new and the resurrected.

This is a great principle pertinent to God's work: that whatever has not been raised from the dead is not workable. After forty long years Moses finally understood that all his former talent, wisdom and power were totally useless. He had gone through death, and now God could give him resurrected courage and ability.

In Exodus 3.12 we find that God promised to be with Moses. In verse 13, however, Moses further inquired: "Behold, when I come unto the children of Israel, and shall say unto them, The God of your fathers hath sent me unto you; and they shall say to me, What is his name? what shall I say unto them?" Here he dared not look upon himself as any longer knowledgeable, as though he could instruct people.

By this time he had been dealt with by God. He neither assumed nor imagined. He dared not move presumptuously. That is why he asked the Lord in such a manner. He had learned his lesson, a lesson not unlike the one the Lord Jesus himself spoke about: "For I spake not from myself; but the Father that sent me, he hath given me a commandment, what I should say, and what I should speak. And I know that his commandment is life eternal: the things therefore which I speak, even as the Father hath said unto me, so I speak" (John 12.49,50).

Moses had come to realize that even the words which he spoke must be commanded by the Lord. How often our words lack the restraint of God. Especially those who are eloquent need His restraint. They fancy they can speak. Yet people who have been dealt with by God know how to be taught in speaking; they dare not rely on themselves. So that even after God told Moses His name, Moses was still afraid to go. He was afraid the children of Israel would not believe his word (Ex. 4.1).

Formerly he had dared to venture out alone and kill an Egyptian, he dared to admonish the two striving Israelites. But here, as the Lord ordered him to go, he trembled and grew fearful. His natural courage had completely vanished. His confidence in himself was entirely gone. He did not believe in himself anymore; he became humble. And his humility almost turned into timidity. Nevertheless, true humility and no confidence in oneself are spiritual manifestations. Moses had now learned the lesson. He knew he could not do anything among the children of Israel by himself. The Lord, therefore, encourage him for the third time. He bestowed upon him the miracle-working power of turning a rod into a serpent, turning water into blood, and afflicting the hand with leprosy. Through these signs the people would believe in him.

Notwithstanding all these signs, however, Moses for the fourth time said: "Oh, Lord, I am not eloquent, neither heretofore, nor since thou hast spoken unto thy servant; for I am slow of speech, and of a slow tongue" (Ex. 4.10). This is totally opposite to the flavor of what is recorded in Acts 7.22, where it is told of how "Moses was instructed in all the wisdom of the Egyptians; and he was mighty in his words and works." Moses was trying to excuse himself by claiming he could not speak since he was not eloquent. Accordingly, the Lord made Aaron Moses' mouth.

Yet further on in the Scriptures we do not find that Aaron spoke to the people for Moses; instead, it was Moses who spoke to them. Why? Because through the many previous years Moses had learned that God had no use for natural eloquence, power and wisdom. Unless the Holy Spirit moves people and gives eloquence, wisdom and power, our natural ability is absolutely useless in the work of God. Spiritual power, though, is altogether necessary.

Do you know after much dealing from the Lord not to use your natural eloquence? You would rather not utter many persuasive words which carry the flavor of little cleverness. Have you received the dealing of the cross and died to your own speech? Without fail our speech will reveal what kind of person we are. God wants us to see that our excellency of speech may not produce fruit nor is it spiritual. If in our speech we are not overcome by God, we will do great damage to His work.

Here we see that Moses made two excuses: first, he was never eloquent but was always slow of speech; and second, even after God had today spoken with him, he still had a slow tongue. He had ruled out himself completely before God. He reckoned that nothing of himself could stand before the Lord. He had truly learned a very deep lesson, for in those forty years he had been delivered from all which was of self and of the natural.

Excessive Withdrawal in His Not Knowing the Power of Resurrection

Knowing one's own uselessness alone is still useless. The important thing is to know the power of God. And that is true resurrection. God had wanted Moses to know that it was He who had made man's mouth. God tried to encourage Moses. "Oh, Lord, send, I pray thee, by the hand of him whom thou wilt send" (Ex. 4.13). Moses again excused himself. When God heard this, He was angry with Moses. And why? Because even though it is of great importance and highly acceptable to God that we are brought to the place of no self-confidence and no self-reliance, nevertheless, if we stay *there* and refuse to go forward by trusting in God, we will greatly displease Him.

How we need to be careful lest we swing from one extreme to the other. Having the promise of God in His granting us eloquence, we will sin against Him if we still do not advance. We should be humble but not draw back, careful but not timid. We must guard against not trusting in God as well as against trusting in self-confidence. God takes us through death in order to raise us up. Death is not the end, resurrection is the goal. We will be of no use if we remain in death and not come into resurrection.

Moses wanted to hide, and he was lazy. He even anticipated that it would be best if God did not send him. Now, it certainly is good to know one's weakness, but not to believe that God is able to strengthen a person is a harmful element in self-knowledge. Excessive judgment of one's weakness like an excessive estimate of one's power can cause one to not trust in God. Many shrinking backs do not constitute spiritual humility, they instead reflect a fear and laziness that stems from looking within oneself. We should on the positive side trust in the mighty power of God and be strong.

It is exceedingly important in spiritual work that there be such a clear transaction with respect to God's commission. The Lord Jesus did not come to this world on His own. The Bible says He was *sent*: the Father sent His Son to the world. Nowadays God's work is damaged by many who volunteer, people who are *not sent* by Him. God does not approve of people who go to work without being sent. He is not pleased with men's presumptuous actions. The sin of presumption is the same as the sin of rebellion. Not to act when ordered is sin; to act without an order is also sin. Moses did not go because he wanted to go. As a matter of fact, he did not even wish to go. But God commanded him to go.

I heard a missionary once say: if we are not able *not* to work for God, we will not be used by Him to save sinners; but if we are able not to work for God's sake, we will be used by Him to save people. This does not mean He is going to save souls without the instrumentality of the preaching of the gospel by men. Nevertheless, if a work is not of God's will, we must be willing not to do it. We must not act presumptuously. Without the command of God, we would rather be quiet than move ahead. And such kind of people will be sent by Him to save souls.

Today the church suffers great loss not because of outside opposition nor because of inside unbelief, but because many who confess to have sound faith move presumptuously without being sent or commanded by God. Thus their works have no spiritual value and reality. To do anything without being sent or ordered is like building a house on the sand or else like gold plating. It may stand temporarily or it may glitter for a while, but it will be destroyed at the judgment seat of Christ. Only those works that closely follow the command of God are useful.

Was Circumcised

Moses at this point said no more. Yet he needed to demonstrate that he had completely denied all that was natural and fleshly by delivering this to death before he could ever go and save the children of

Israel. And hence we read that "it came to pass on the way at the lodging-place, that Jehovah met him, and sought to kill him" (Ex. 4.24). Why such action by God? Because Moses was not under the sign of the covenant. Moses and his sons had not been circumcised. This made them the same as Gentiles. Soon he would begin to do God's work, and yet he was still as an uncircumcised Gentile. God could not let him go and deliver the children of Israel. He therefore sought to kill Moses in order to show him that His divine work could not be done by an uncircumcised person. Thus circumcision was performed. And after this was done, he was allowed to go and save the Israelites.* Later on when the children of Israel came to the first station in Canaan, they too received the rite of circumcision.

What is the meaning of circumcision? "In whom ye were also circumcised with a circumcision not made with hands, in the putting off of the body of the flesh, in the circumcision of Christ" (Col. 2.11). This verse plainly tells us that circumcision has no other meaning but the putting off of the flesh. What is the flesh? It is all that we are naturally endowed with at the time of birth: "That which is born of the flesh is flesh; and that which is born of the Spirit is spirit" (John 3.6). Everything we have before our regeneration is the flesh. What we have after being born again is spiritual. Natural eloquence, power, wisdom,

---

*From the record of Exodus 4.25, it would seem that only Moses' son was circumcised. Moses was probably circumcised on the eighth day by his parents back in Egypt.—*Translator*

cleverness and good works are all of the flesh. What must we now do? By the cross of Christ we should cut off all these natural specialties. We must deny our natural eloquence or power or wisdom. And such is the circumcision spoken of in Colossians chapter 2.

The work of God can only be done by those whom He has slain. The flesh has no place for itself but death in the sight of God. All who follow the flesh are marked by Him for slaughter. The work of God demands the very death of the natural man.

4. The Principle of the Cross

Have you died? Have you forsaken your natural talents? If you have not done so, you are not qualified to do God's work. Nowadays many are working, but they are not doing *God's* work. Because it is not God who is working, then it is men who are doing so. It is not the new creation at work, the old creation is at work. So that the Holy Spirit does not work at all. To work by the power of the Holy Spirit is to work from spirit to spirit—that is to say, from your spirit reaching out to the spirit of other people.

Why does Paul refuse to preach the word of the cross with excellency of speech? Lest the word of the cross become ineffectual, for the cross is a fact. If you preach it with fleshly knowledge, you can only spread its reason. You have not spread its power and life. This is because you preach the cross without having the Spirit of the cross as well as the life of the cross. You do not preach according to the principle of the cross, and therefore you can only see the reason (or logic) of the cross being propagated and not its power. Because of this, the cross must become a kind of principle to us first.

We need to inquire as to what qualifies us to preach the cross? Do we do this work because we are deeply familiar with Bible doctrines, or that we are capable of expounding them with eloquence, or because preaching is our profession? How pitiful if such be the case. Many leaders become such in the church not because of their spiritual experience and the life and power of the Holy Spirit—actually many who listen to our preaching have better spiritual life, deeper experience, and more understanding in spiritual things than we who preach. In some places I have often seen young workers teaching older people who have little knowledge. Yet the fact of the matter is that these older people far exceed these younger workers in spiritual experience, faith and prayer. But solely because these younger people have a little knowledge and a little eloquence, they venture to teach the older ones in spiritual things.

We ought to know whether or not God has dealt with us. Has my natural talent been dealt with? Is God powerful in me? Without such deeper experience, I will only be telling people in my own ability that this is how they must walk, though I myself am totally ignorant of the way. How many today are the blind leading the blind! Many preachers know only how to propagate knowledge; they are not able to supply divine life and the Holy Spirit.

Hence the problem lies in the principle. A grain of wheat remains a solitary entity unless it dies. If your cleverness and natural ability have not died, you are of no use to God. For in spiritual things it is not a question of wisdom and cleverness, nor a matter of a good mind and understanding, but a concern to have experience and power in the spirit.

If after a person is saved he experiences deeply spiritual realities, he will have no need for people to revive him. Many travel around and lead meetings in the power of their natural wisdom. Do they not realize just how much they need God to revive them? If He does not revive them, then all their works shall be in vain. And other people will receive nothing as well. So that God must bring us to our end.

I would rather quit preaching if I have to continue forward preaching only in my own strength. What must be the future result if such kind of preaching is done for thirty years? What must surely happen at the judgment seat of Christ? God would rather have us receive the light of the judgment seat beforehand so that we would confess our error and cease doing it again.

May God enlighten us to perceive how wrong it is for us to work with our knowledge and natural ability so that we will reckon all that is of the old Adamic creation to be dead. We will reject all of that just as we did at the time of our salvation. Let us truly deny all that is of the old creation and receive new life from Christ's new creation. And let us seriously ask ourselves how our way and future are determined. Are they decided by God's will and power or by our own self life?

Some people get revived after each revival meeting

they attend. But after the meeting is over, their revival is also over. Such kind of revival is like injecting a stimulant, the dosage of which must be increased the second time around for it to continue to work. Since on the first occasion they were revived through outside enthusiasm and emotion, now they shall require even better eloquence and even more excitement on the second occasion to revive them—or else they will not be revived at all.

May God really obtain something in us for His name. If He does not obtain anything, He is not glorified. All ends in vanity. May we be so dealt with by God that we become all His, and that we may render to Him what He deserves to have. May we commit ourselves with simpleness of heart into His hand and wait for His leading. Were God already leading you, all you would need would be to deny completely your own wisdom and power and receive afresh from Him new power. Examine whether or not your way is truly appointed by God.

We want to see the Lord glorified and His will done. We want Him, not us, to have possession. We shall never manage our life and work with fleshly wisdom. We shall only ask whether we are doing God's will. Have we done His will? Let us have no will of our own but take His will as ours.

8 | Poor Indeed

Because thou sayest, I am rich, and have gotten riches, and have need of nothing; and knowest not that thou art the wretched one and miserable and poor and blind and naked. (Rev. 3.17)

One

A very real problem is often found among God's children. It is "the attitude and mind of Laodicea." This attitude of mind is reflected in people thinking themselves spiritually rich when they are actually very poor.

In spiritual matters it is rather easy to solve the problem of have or have not, but it is not an easy thing to resolve the question of whether one is rich or poor. He who has nothing can easily find God, but he who is poor has difficulty in meeting Him. Many really have nothing before God, and yet they are frequently met by Him. The worst person is he who says he has, and he does indeed have something. If you mention one thing, he declares he knows; if you speak of another thing, again he knows. But does he really know? Not at all. He says he has so much, yet he hardly moves a step forward. He is truly a poor man.

The biggest problem with a poor man is that he does not easily recognize his poverty. The one who has nothing will readily confess his nothingness. If he has, he has; and if he has nothing, he has nothing. This is quite simple to understand and easily shown. But poverty is something relative: A may not be as rich as B, A may be poorer than B. B may not be as rich as C, and B may be poorer than C. Hence it is rather difficult to conclude who is the poor one.

When a child gets his first allowance, he thinks he has more money than anybody else in the world. He does not truly know his poverty, however. If he has nothing, he readily sees he has nothing; but having a little makes it hard for him to understand the insufficiency of what he has. In spiritual things, God has a way with him who has absolutely none; but in the case of the poor, his little will hinder him because it creates unwarranted self-conceit and self-satisfaction.

Someone during the past decades may have obeyed God three times. He can never forget how previously he had obeyed God. Yet while he is talking about obedience, those who have really learned the lesson of obedience and who are sensitive in their spirit will rise up and say: "What do *you* know of obedience?" For that man is a poor man, he is truly poverty-stricken!

There are some other people who like to talk about the cross. "A" says a person needs the cross before God, and "B" says he certainly needs the cross. But those who really know the cross will say, "Brethren, do you know what the cross is?" Do not imagine because you have been dealt with by the Lord a few times that your self has been touched. Do realize that the first day in which you were saved and were dealt with by God does not mean that you have already learned a very deep lesson. You are far from it. The one who mentions the cross frequently and yet knows it not is a truly poor person.

Some brother may say he is clear in his understanding about the church, for as he perceives the body of Christ, he acts and reacts accordingly. Some sister may say she is one who seeks the kingdom since she is willing to lay down everything for the kingdom's sake. Those who know them will nonetheless say that neither he nor she knows the body or the kingdom. Many of God's children possess a cheap obedience, a cheap cross, and a cheap kingdom. They do not know in reality what obedience, the cross and the kingdom are. This we call poverty.

Two

Poverty without pride is not an absolute obstacle to spiritual progress. But poverty which falls into pride creates an impossible situation. Poverty itself is not the problem, and yet *Laodicea* is a problem because she is not only poor but also proud, not merely poor but also considering herself rich. How few are those who are poor and not proud in spiritual things; the rich, though, are usually not proud. Is it not sad that many of God's children are circling around without making real progress because their self-conceit has damaged them? Many are talking about the flesh, though they are really ignorant of what the flesh is. Many are speaking of revelation and yet they do not know what revelation basically is. They have much to say about obedience, about the kingdom, and even about how the cross deals with the natural life of man; nevertheless, in their very talking they expose themselves as being quite poor and ignorant. For they have yet to touch God. When people speak on things they do not experience, they can only deceive themselves and those who are like them. In spiritual things, therefore, a person who styles himself as being rich will never convince others that he is rich; to the contrary, he will be recognized as poor.

"I am rich, and have gotten riches, and have need of nothing," declares the church in Laodicea. (These riches do not point to material but to spiritual things.) She feels she *has* achieved riches, yet God declares, "Knowest not that thou art the wretched one and miserable and poor and blind and naked"? Do you have anything? You most likely *do* have a few things, but what you have has not had much effect in your life. If you genuinely have them, you *should* be joyful; but unfortunately, you are wretched and miserable. You do not give the appearance of one who possesses. Your wretchedness and misery betray to people the fact that you are poor.

Poverty is closely related to blindness. He who is poor is unable to see into spiritual things. He who does not see usually deems himself to be rich. He who does not see the cross will think that he has the cross, he who does not see the kingdom will believe he has the kingdom and he who has never known the body of Christ will assume he knows the church. Whosoever therefore reckons himself as possessing is actually a poor man spiritually. Whenever we truly perceive, we will not boast that we are rich. Whenever anyone's eyes are opened, he will see his nakedness and acknowledge it. Only the foolish one will brag that he possesses. Being poor and yet not realizing his poverty makes of him a Laodicean. And just this is what we all need to be warned about.

Three

What is poverty? Poverty is not a matter of quantity. It is rather a matter of quality. 1 Corinthians 3 shows us the difference between gold, silver and precious stones on the one hand, and wood, hay and stubble on the other. 2 Timothy 2 speaks of the vessels of gold and silver and the vessels of wood and earth. This clearcut disparity in description tells us which is rich and which is poor. Hence even if you *have,* you need to see exactly what you *do* have. If you have a large pile of wood, hay and stubble, you are yet poor. Having a vessel is not enough to know; the question must be asked whether it is a wooden and earthen vessel or one of gold and silver. How easy for us to be proud because we feel we have something. We think as long as we have something, we are in an excellent state. But let us realize that if we do not know what we have, we are numbered among the poor.

Viewing this whole issue from still another angle, poverty can also be said to be shallowness, infantilism, and immaturity. An abundant life is a matured life. We know the difference between growing and arriving at maturity. A child will grow annually; but after he comes of age, it is no longer a matter of growth, but is to him a matter of maturity. He who only experiences the period of growing does not have abundant life; it requires the time of maturing to achieve abundance. All who deem the beginning to be the whole will consider themselves fully possessing everything. And as such they are today's Laodiceans: they are the spiritually poor. How harmful, then, initial experiences can be to entering into deeper experiences. A shallow experience may hinder us from having a truly deep experience; having superficial knowledge may hamper us from having deeper knowledge.

Four

Abundance is not a matter of merely having or having not; it is primarily a matter of *what* we have, of how *much* we have, and how *deep*. Abundance is not an initial experience; neither is it a mental understanding of the teaching on the abundant life nor its elucidation. Abundance is rather a being brought by

God one day into divinely seeing, thus entering into the realm of spiritual abundance.

A brother during the first year of his salvation spent much time in searching the Scriptures. He studied especially concerning the second coming of the Lord. He managed to analyze the events surrounding the Lord's return. And as a result, he felt fairly proud of himself. One day he met a sister who had deep experience with the Lord. They conversed together on the second coming. She, however, did not analyze as he did. What she stressed was how to wait for the Lord's return. On that day, that brother learned a deep lesson. He had been one who *talked* about the second coming of the Lord Jesus, but here was another person who was *waiting* for the Lord's return. Whoever merely talks about Jesus' second coming is poor, whereas the one who waits for the Lord's return is quite rich.

All who have really seen before God will not dare to be self-complacent. For example, to really perceive Romans 6 may take one, two, ten or twenty times of reading. When you first read Romans 6, you may feel good about it and declare that you have seen it. But when you read it the second time, you will say, "Alas, I had not really seen it before." This shows that when light comes, it destroys what you had held originally. There was once a brother who knew about the church quite well. On one occasion when several people had together received some light on the church, he announced, "How strange; I had never really known the church before. But thank God, today I *see* it."

Others might have thought, because of his previous knowledge, that if *he* did not know the church, who else could know the church! Yet as he later received divine light, he saw that he actually had nothing. For when light enlightens, it devours. The greater light will swallow up the lesser light. All lesser lights will be lost in the greater light. Each time one truly sees something before God, he feels as if he had never seen. This does not mean that he has literally seen nothing before, because he could very well *have* seen something in the past; it only means that when he subsequently receives greater light, it will be to him as if that which he saw before pales by comparison with this new light, and he will be only conscious now of his having nothing!

Abundance comes from enlightenment. As light shines upon us, we become rich. Yet strange to say, when we do receive such enlightening, we feel on our side as though decreased and not increased. For the shining of light will break up your past sight. It destroys what you originally had. Under the illumination of God, we actually do increase, and yet we do not feel it that way! So that what in the sight of God actually is, and what is our own feeling, are two different things. As God gives light, if you think you have increased then in reality you have seen nothing. But in case you indeed see, then you will feel as though you have just been saved and have only begun. It should not be inferred from this that you were not saved before; it simply signifies that so far as your feeling is concerned, you sense an emptiness as though you had never commenced walking on the spiritual pathway of life. One who is truly abundant senses himself to be nothing under the light of God.

Our God is the God of abundance. He does not wish His children to be poor. The works He desires are not those of wood, hay and stubble. The vessels He uses are not wooden and earthen vessels. Being the God of riches, He will only use rich vessels. His riches are deep and abundant: "There shall not be room enough to receive it" (Mal. 3.10). Such is His grace! Whatever He does in our lives is superabundant. It is never forced or weak or small. Oh, this God of abundance can make us rich because He always gives more. And each time He gives more, we feel as if it is the very first time of our receiving *anything*. Although it seems strange, yet how true it is.

May God have mercy upon us that we may indeed see light. The proud man is foolish for he is poor. May God empty us that we may enter into His abundance.

9 The Significance of Faith

When the fulness of the time came, God sent forth his son, born of a woman, born under the law, that he might redeem them that were under the law, that we might receive the adoption of sons. (Gal. 4.4,5)

So belief cometh of hearing, and hearing by the word of Christ. (Rom. 10.17)

Without faith it is impossible to be well-pleasing unto [God]. (Heb. 11.6)

Because ye are sons, God sent forth the Spirit of his Son into our hearts, crying, Abba, Father. (Gal. 4.6)

The Comforter, even the Holy Spirit, whom the Father will send in my name, he shall teach you all things, and bring to your remembrance all that I said unto you. (John 14.26)

Howbeit when he, the Spirit of truth, is come, he shall guide you into all the truth. (John 16.13)

Today I sense deeply the need of preaching to you

a special message on the significance of faith. "Without faith it is impossible to be well-pleasing unto [God]," declares Hebrews 11.6. We know that the most important thing in a Christian's life is to be well-pleasing to God. Yet he cannot please Him without having faith. Why is faith so significant? If we were to go through a concordance on the word "faith" we would find that all the grace which God has provided for men is given to them through faith. Faith is so essential that God will not give grace for any other reason. Why is it that many people seem to be quite obedient and willing to do good, yet they do not receive much of God's grace? We need to realize that in God's way of redemption, there are four essentials:

(1) *The work of Christ.* The first step is having Christ's accomplished redemption for us. Through His own death and resurrection, He has completed the work of redemption for us.

(2) *The word of God.* Through His word God tells us what He has done for us men. The word of God spreads the news concerning the accomplished work of Christ.

(3) *Men believing God's word.* What we believe is the word of God, not the work of Christ. His work has satisfied the heart of God. He has accomplished what God has purposed. What we trust in is the work of Christ, but what we believe in is the word of God. For without the word of God we cannot place our trust in the work of Christ. Without God's word, we have no knowledge of Christ's work. Hence believing God's word is trusting in Christ's work.

(4) *The Holy Spirit working into believers the fin-*

ished work of Christ. When the Bible mentions the Holy Spirit, it puts special emphasis on the communion of the Holy Spirit because it is the Spirit who channels the finished work of Christ into us as well as leads us into the truth of God. Truth is reality, that is, spiritual reality. The Biblical conception of truth is twofold: (a) truth points to Christ and to that which He has accomplished, for the Lord says, "I am the truth" (John 14.6); and (b) it points to the word of God, because Christ also declares: "thy word is truth" (John 17.17). The Holy Spirit is the Spirit of truth. It is He who causes us to enter into Christ and all that Christ has done for us. It is also He who makes God's word real in our lives.

Now such being God's way of redemption, no one may receive anything without faith. Although Christ has accomplished all and God's word has testified to it, the Holy Spirit can do nothing and we will receive nothing if we do not believe.

How much does the work of Christ include? Some time ago, when a few sisters were baptized, I spoke on the riches in Christ. Sanctification, perfection, end of condemnation, deliverance from sin, holiness, God's pleasure, and so forth—all these have been achieved by Christ. When He died, you too died in Him. When He was resurrected, you also were resurrected in Him. When He ascended, you ascended in Him as well. You do not seek to die, for this Christ has already died for you. You may be told—when you are spiritually or morally weak—that you need to die and then you will sin no more; but the word of God tells you that about 2000 years ago you had already died. What you cannot do yourself, Christ has already done for you.

No sinner can be saved by works. One day he understands that salvation is on the basis of the work of Christ, and so he enters into rest. Today many Christians are in a dilemma. They appear to be unable to die. Today they are bad, and tomorrow they will still be bad. No matter how much they try to be good, they try in vain. Oh, let me say that it is an erroneous gospel if it calls upon you *to do it yourself.* The Bible explicitly states *this:* "In [Christ] ye were also circumcised with a circumcision not made with hands, in the putting off of the body of the flesh, in the circumcision of Christ" (Col. 2.11). All is done for us by Christ This is His work. We ought to reckon what has been done in Him.

What the Lord Jesus has accomplished is to cause us to be perfect in Him; and the Holy Spirit incorporates within us everything which is in Christ. He has not only died but has also been resurrected. When Christ died, we also died; when He was resurrected, we also were resurrected; and when He ascended, we also ascended. Our inheritance in Him is in fact far beyond our expectation.

When we read the Bible we must take note of this point: are we going to obtain what is in Christ or have we already obtained it? Once I told a brother to read Romans 6 and learn how much he ought to do and how much he had already obtained with regard to death and resurrection. His answer was that he must die and be resurrected. I assured him that my Bible did not say that, for Romans 6 in my Bible states that he had already died and been resurrected; and that therefore all he needed to do was to consecrate himself to God.

People in this world also talk about death and resurrection, but they have no basis for the fulfillment of these. We thank God, that Christ has already accomplished everything. Yet how can we believe unless the Bible—the word of God—has told us that Christ has already died and been resurrected? Through the Scriptures we come into the knowledge of what Christ has done. For this reason, what we believe is God's word and not Christ's work. How can we believe since we were not eyewitnesses to the death of Christ? We can believe because the word of God tells us so. God commanded His servants to write down all that Christ had accomplished in His dying and being raised from the dead for us. And this gives us the ground of faith.

Believing God's word is most essential. "He that believeth on the Son," says the Scripture, "hath eternal life" (John 3.36). When the Bible talks about "believing in Me," "believing in My name," etc., what is it that we must believe? In believing in the Lord Jesus, does it mean to believe in His work? "Belief cometh of hearing, and hearing by the word of Christ" (Rom. 10.17). If there is no word, what can we believe? God's word brings near to us that which is far away. Unless we lay hold of God's word, we have not believed. Without God's word, our faith shall be groundless; it will but be psychological.

What is the difference between faith and psychology? Psychology is to make believe what is not said, whereas faith is believing what has been said. For example, nobody has invited me to eat dinner tonight, but I say I believe Mr. So-and-So has invited me for dinner tonight. This is nothing but psychology operating; it certainly is not faith, since Mr. So-and-So has not stated such an invitation. But if somebody has indeed said he invites me to have dinner with him tonight, and I thus believe he has invited me to dinner, then that is faith because he has said so. Hence in spiritual matters we must have the word of God before we can believe. We have not seen ourselves crucified by God; that is done by God himself. And so we need God to tell us that we have been crucified, and then we can believe it.

How do we know that the word of God is true? Because *what God has done is true.* What He says simply reflects what He has already done. As an illustration of this, let us suppose that I went to the park yesterday. Today I tell you that yesterday I was in the park. Since my visit to the park was real and true, what I say about it is also real and true. The work of Christ is finished, and the word of God tells us what Christ has accomplished. We therefore believe, and it becomes ours. We do not need to do anything but believe in God's word. Without it there can be no faith.

Faith is believing the word of God. It is the most difficult thing to do in the world and yet it is also the easiest thing to do in the world. Is this paradoxical? Yes, and yet it is quite true. Frequently we cannot believe; but the moment we do believe, all is ours. This is borne out by our experience.

J. Wilbur Chapman had at one time preached in Shanghai, and his work was very effective. Although at a certain point in his career he had already become a doctor of divinity, he was not saved. Once after a meeting was over, D. L. Moody invited him for a talk. "Dr. Chapman, are you a saved Christian? Do you belong to Christ?" "I dare not say I am, though I hope I may belong to Him," replied Chapman. So Moody read John 3.16 with him. At the end of his reading, Moody asked him again, "Dr. Chapman, are you a saved Christian? Do you belong to Christ?" He still replied, "I dare not say, but I most eagerly hope I am." Whereupon Moody read John 3.16 once more.

After he finished reading it a second time, he looked at Chapman intently. Chapman felt so embarrassed by Moody's look that he muttered aloud: "I really hope I may say I belong to Christ." Moody then spoke with great sincerity, "Dr. Chapman, do you know whose word you are now doubting?" Immediately Chapman was awakened to reality and he realized that he had been doubting the word of God.

Afterwards, throughout his entire life, Chapman continually testified that whatever God had said, that for him was it. Initially he had thought he had had to do better in order to be qualified for heaven. But now he realized that God has said: "he that believeth on the Son hath eternal life" (John 3.36); so that whoever believes has eternal life indeed.

Let us reckon with this fact, that God has already accomplished all things for us in Christ; we therefore believe, and therefore we possess. To believe in God's word means nothing more nor less than to believe precisely as God has said.

In America there was once a president of a Bible school. He had been able to overcome many things in his life except for four or five sins which he committed repeatedly. He confessed that his history was a story of continual confession. One day he read Romans 6.14: "Sin shall not have dominion over you: for ye are not under law, but under grace." He accordingly prayed as follows: "Your word says sin shall not have dominion over me, but my situation attests that sin *has had* dominion over me. Nevertheless, today I believe in Your word, therefore I declare I have already overcome my sin." Later on, when one of the same temptations came his way, he would still fall if he looked at himself; but whenever he trusted in the word of God, telling God that His word could not be untrue, he experienced victory. And thus he lived a victorious life. Here is the most important thing for us to lay hold of: God's word. If you look at yourself, you shall be as corrupted as you were before. If you look at your environment, it will be as difficult as it has always been. But if you believe in God's word, you are able to overcome.

There was once a woman who was extremely weak physically. She had a son of sixteen, bad and uncontrollable. One day she prayed to God: "I cannot bear such a heavy burden any longer. Please give me a promise." She received what she asked for in Philippians 4.6 and 7: "In nothing be anxious; but in everything by prayer and supplication with thanksgiving let your requests be made known unto God. And the peace of God, which passeth all understanding, shall guard your hearts and your thoughts in Christ Jesus." She believed God that it would be even as it had been spoken to her. However, her son went from bad to worse as time went on.

One day, she suddenly was notified by the police that her son was at the station because he had been run over by a car. She went to the police station and found her son in a very bloody state. Her husband had also come along, and he fainted when he saw his son's bloody condition. Other relatives arrived as well. Yet they all wondered why she could remain smiling under such trying circumstances. Was her heart so hard? "No," she said, "for God has promised in His word to give me peace that passes all understanding. And today I meet up with this accident, but I have been given the peace which surpasses understanding. Therefore I can be calm." Faith is a laying hold of God's word.

If I meet a patient and ask him how he is, I may get an answer from him that he believes God will eventually heal him. Yet I know God will not heal him because he does not have God's word. One brother was nearsighted and intended to get a pair of spectacles. Someone told him he should believe God and not wear spectacles. Now he had come to consider his faith to be stronger than that of other people. And so he prayed. Later on he was invited to preach the gospel. He thought his eyesight would be restored after preaching. He even asked me to pray with him. I told him frankly that I could predict God would not heal him. He asked why. I said because he did not have God's word, and therefore his faith was not faith but feeling. What he was professing to have was in fact not faith but hope. How can anyone believe if there is not the word of God present?

The work of Christ is real, yet the whole world will still perish if there is not the word of God. With the presence of the word of God, though, even the whole world cannot overturn what you and I believe. Once long ago our Lord had ordered His disciples as follows: "Let us go over *unto the other side.*" Whereupon He went to sleep in the stern of the boat. Suddenly there arose a great storm of wind, and the waves beat high upon the boat so much that it was now filling up with water. The disciples awakened the Lord, saying, "Teacher, carest thou not that we perish?" He then rose up and rebuked the wind; and the wind ceased, and there was a great calm. Afterwards, what did He say to the disciples? "Why are ye fearful? have ye not yet faith?" (see Mark 4.35–41) Since the Lord had commanded to go to the other side, He *will* be responsible, no matter what happens on the way—be it storm or wave. Not believing what the Lord has spoken is nothing less than discounting His word. Suppose, for instance, that I give you a ten-dollar bill to have changed. How do you know you are entitled to receive ten dollars' worth of change? Because the correct amount of value is printed on the ten-dollar bill. So too is it with divine things, for whatever amount God says there is, the exact amount shall be forthcoming. Whatever God says is true. If the Lord commands you to go to the other side, to the other side you will go. You can bravely challenge the wind to blow and the wave to roar, for you will still get to the other side because you believe that the Lord has said so. But if you doubt His word, you shall indeed sink to the bottom of the sea through the opposition of the wind and the waves.

The word of God alone is true. Even if circumstances should all be against you, His word remains true. When you have problems with your home, school, business or personal needs, your prayers will be in vain if you do not believe God's word. You have not, because you pray not. You pray and still have not, because you do not believe in God's word (cf. James 4.2,3). It is a waste of time to pray without believing in the word of God. In order to receive God's grace, one thing which is so necessary is to lay hold of His word. You believe and God performs. Whenever something confronts you, you must ask Him to give you a word. And then with His word, you shall be able to break through any problem whatsoever. To have God's word in such a manner is to possess the sword of the Spirit. Almost all the armor mentioned in Ephesians 6 is for defensive purposes; only the sword of the Holy Spirit, "which is the word of God," is for offensive use. Having God's word, you can overthrow every obstacle and solve all problems.

I had a friend who once had spent her last penny. During that time she read the Bible and prayed: "O God, give me a word. I do not ask you to place a thousand dollars before me. I only want you to give me a word." God caused her to recall a statement in Psalm 23: "my cup runneth over" (v.5). At that moment, she was not only unfilled but literally empty. Yet she believed God's word and wrote the following poem:

There is always something over,
When we trust our gracious Lord;
Every cup He fills o'erfloweth,
His great rivers all are broad.
Nothing narrow, nothing stinted,
Ever issued from His store;
To His own He gives full measure,
Running over, evermore.

There is always something over,
When we, from the Father's hand,
Take our portion with thanksgiving,
Praising for the path He planned.
Satisfaction, full and deepening,
Fills the soul, and lights the eye,
When the heart has trusted Jesus
All its need to satisfy.

There is always something over,
When we tell of all His love;
Unplumbed depths still lie beneath us,
Unscaled heights rise far above.
Human lips can never utter
All His wondrous tenderness.
We can only praise and wonder,
And His name forever bless.

—Margaret E. Barber

She sent this poem to a friend. After a while her friend wrote back and said this: "Having read your poem, I imagine God must have really blessed you so that you have so much left over." Yet who knew that she did not even have a penny? But did the word of God fall short? Not at all, for after two days God supplied her need through some human instrument.

Oh, if you have the word of God, you have an inexhaustible source of supply. The ravens will supply your needs, the brook will also supply you; even the handful of a widow's meal will also be your supply (see 1 Kings 17). And if there is neither raven nor brook nor widow, God will open the window of heaven and give you supply from above. This is faith.

The work of Christ is done, and the word of God has also declared it. I believe, and so I have everything. The Spirit of God's word is the Holy Spirit. Whoever believes in God's word, the Holy Spirit is responsible to put into that one the reality of God's word. If you believe, then the Holy Spirit will lead you into Christ and into all He has accomplished. The work of Christ is finished and the word of God is given; but the Holy Spirit cannot apply to you what Christ has accomplished if you do not believe.

Why is it that having seen and understood what God has accomplished in Christ, we still do not possess our possession? It is because we have no faith. We may say we have believed, yet why do we not receive? May I say that in point of fact we have *not* believed, else if we had truly believed, the Holy Spirit would have been responsible to translate our belief into reality. Knowing alone is not enough; faith must be added to knowledge. Oftentimes we read an entire chapter of the Bible, and yet we most probably have not believed even one verse of it. We lack faith in many things. The moment we believe, however, the

Holy Spirit immediately accomplishes in us what we believe.

When God says, Let there be light, there is light indeed. Whatever God speaks, it is done in the universe. In the beginning God spoke, and the universe obeyed Him. Today He continues to speak, and the universe still obeys; for every word of God has power in it. And the power behind the word is the Holy Spirit. As God speaks, the Holy Spirit instantly accomplishes what God has said.

This is equally true with sinners being saved. As soon as a sinner believes in the word of God, the Holy Spirit immediately gives him that which Christ has accomplished. The opium smoker or the helpless drunkard finds deliverance as he believes in God's word. The habit of smoking or drinking is cut off as by a sword. This is none other than the Holy Spirit giving that person the power to overcome.

I once had a classmate who according to his nature was most crafty. He could wrap the entire class around his little finger because all his classmates were afraid of him. Later he was converted to Christ and became my fellow-worker. Not knowing his past, no one would ever have dreamed that he had been that kind of person before. He was what he now was purely because of the power of resurrection.

The wonder of wonders in this world is that a dead person may receive God's life. As soon as anyone believes, the Holy Spirit will put in him all which Christ has accomplished. He may say "I believe" as he is listening to the preaching of God's word or perhaps as he sits in the last row of the auditorium or even as he is walking on the street. And just when he believes, at that very moment the Holy Spirit communicates to him what Christ has accomplished.

My responsibility has been to deliver this message to you. It is well if you believe. May God work in our midst, causing us to believe His word just as it was written.

10 Four Significant Stages in Life's Journey

And it came to pass, when Jehovah would take up Elijah by a whirlwind into heaven, that Elijah went with Elisha from Gilgal. And Elijah said unto Elisha, Tarry here, I pray thee; for Jehovah hath sent me as far as Bethel. And Elisha said, As Jehovah liveth, and as thy soul liveth, I will not leave thee. So they went down to Bethel. . . . And Elijah said unto him, Elisha, Tarry here, I pray thee; for Jehovah hath sent me to Jericho. And he said, As Jehovah liveth, and as thy soul liveth, I will not leave thee. So they came to Jericho . . . And Elijah said unto him, Tarry here, I pray thee; for Jehovah hath sent me to the Jordan. And he said, As Jehovah liveth, and as thy soul liveth, I will not leave thee. And they two went on. . . . And Elijah took his mantle, and wrapped it together, and smote the waters, and they were divided hither and thither, so that they two went over on dry ground. And it came to pass, when they were gone over, that Elijah said unto Elisha, Ask what I shall do for thee, before I am taken from thee. And

> Elisha said, I pray thee, let a double portion of thy spirit be upon me. . . . And it came to pass, as they still went on, and talked, that, behold, there appeared a chariot of fire and horses of fire, which parted them both asunder; and Elijah went up by a whirlwind into heaven. . . . He took up also the mantle of Elijah that fell from him, and went back, and stood by the bank of the Jordan. And he took the mantle of Elijah that fell from him, and smote the waters, and said, Where is Jehovah, the God of Elijah? and when he also had smitten the waters, they were divided hither and thither; and Elisha went over. (2 Kings 2.1–14)

In this passage of Scripture, we find delineated for us four stages in a particular journey; it started from Gilgal, proceeded onward to Bethel, went next to Jericho, and finally crossed over the Jordan River.

At the time when Elijah was going to be taken up to heaven and when Elisha was soon to receive a double portion of the Holy Spirit, these two men of God traveled along a pathway which connected these four locations. From the physical and geographical we can derive a very important spiritual lesson here—which is, that if we wish to be raptured to heaven like Elijah or to receive the Holy Spirit as a mantle like Elisha, we must travel through these same four stages of life as are typified for us by these four places in their journey. Whether we look forward to being raptured or we expect to receive the power of the Holy Spirit, we too must commence a journey at Gilgal and travel forward until we also cross the river Jordan. Let us now see exactly what these four places can represent.

1. Gilgal (v.1)—Dealing with the Flesh

In order to interpret correctly the meaning of Gilgal, we first must understand the principle of first mention in the Scriptures. We learn from Joshua 5.9 (the clearest earliest reference as to its meaning) that Gilgal as a place name means "rolled away." From reading verses 2 through 9 we understand that the generation of the children of Israel who initially came out of Egypt were all circumcised, but that the generation of Israelites who were afterwards born in the wilderness were not circumcised. This latter generation were now at this time entering Canaan. They would soon inherit their inheritance. Therefore the old flesh must be "rolled away"; the reproach of Egypt must be put off or removed from them, that they might have a change towards a new life; for the meaning of circumcision, as revealed to us in the New Testament, is "the putting off of the body of the flesh" (Col. 2.11).

Who truly recognizes what the flesh is? Who understands what is meant by dealing with the flesh? or the judging of the flesh? Many people deem victory over sin to be the hallmark of perfection. Yet they do not know that there is the flesh which sins! According to the Scriptures, "the flesh" is condemned by God. It is something with which God is most displeased. The flesh is everything we have through birth: "That which is born of the flesh is flesh'' (John 3.6). Whatever we have by birth is of the flesh, and includes not only sin and uncleanness and corruption but also natural goodness, ability, zeal, wisdom and power. A most difficult lesson to be learned in a believer's life is for that one to know his own flesh. The Christian must be brought through all kinds of failures and deprivations before he knows what his flesh is.

What hinders a believer's progress the most in life and work is his flesh. He is unaware of God's calling him to deny his entire flesh. He imagines that forsaking sins is quite enough. He is ignorant of God's equal displeasure with his own ability, zeal and wisdom in God's work and his own goodness and power in spiritual life. Whatever we reckon as good according to the flesh, whatever we plan and ingeniously arrange by means of the flesh is something we must deny, deliver up to death, and allow to pass through judgment according to God. The Lord has no use for the help of the flesh, neither in spiritual life nor in spiritual work.

Now Gilgal in Joshua's time was precisely the place where the physical flesh was cut off and judged. And for the believer today, in type it is the place where the flesh must be judged by the light God gives to us. God declares that the flesh must be put off; let us agree with Him. He declares it must be circumcised; let us therefore be circumcised in heart. In our spiritual journey through life we too must start from Gilgal and deny the flesh. But please note that this does not specify the degree of one's cutting away; it merely declares that the flesh must be judged. The current error is for people to look for zeal and good works but to overlook the denial of the flesh. Yet what is more essential for them to do is to judge the flesh as God has judged it.

According to very personal experience with the Lord, the highest expression of spiritual life is not regeneration, sanctification, perfection, victory over sin, or power. It is instead the denying of the flesh, which is both the aim and the way of spiritual life. Those who have not started out from Gilgal have never really commenced their spiritual journey. Those who do not learn how to deny the flesh do not know what true spiritual life is. Such persons may be zealous in good works and may be quite happy in doing so, but they have no conception of real spiritual life.

2. Bethel (vv.2,3)—Dealing with the World

From Gilgal we have now come in our journey to Bethel. What is meant by the place name of Bethel? Again let us discover where it is first mentioned in the Bible, and thus we can decipher its meaning for us today. Please read Genesis 12.8. Bethel was the place where Abraham built an altar. An altar is for the purpose of communication with God, of offering sacrifices to God, and of being wholly given to Him.

Genesis 12.9–14 records the descending of Abraham to Egypt. *There* he built *no* altar. His communication with God was thus interrupted, and his heart of consecration was set aside. This marks the difference between Bethel and Egypt. Bethel, therefore, signifies all that is contrary to whatever Egypt stands for.

What Genesis 13.3,4 records is very meaningful: "And he went on his journeys from the south even to Bethel, unto the place where his tent had been at the beginning, between Bethel and Ai, unto the place of the altar, which he had made there at the *first:* and there Abram *called on the name of Jehovah.*" Abraham had had no fellowship with God while he was in Egypt. It was when he returned to the original location—which is to say, to Bethel—that he once again called on the name of the Lord. Only at spiritual Bethel will people commune with God and give themselves to Him.

Hence, whereas Gilgal speaks of our overcoming the flesh, Bethel speaks of our overcoming the world, because Egypt in Scripture represents the world. Overcoming the world is a condition for rapture and for the power of the Holy Spirit. Our lives must reach a point where the world is unable to touch our heart. How much are we in fact separated from it? Do we express through our lives that we are separated? Do our attitudes and words show that we no longer belong to this world? What about our intentions? Do we cherish some secret desire for the things of the world? Do we still surreptitiously look for the praise of men? Do we allow ourselves to suffer a great deal inwardly because of the libel of men? When we incur loss, do we feel that loss intensely? Is there any difference between our feeling towards the world and that of the people of the world themselves?

If our heart has not completely overcome the world, if the people, things and events of this world have not lost their place in us, we will not be able to arrive at our goal. A believer must pay the price in following the Lord if he expects to be filled with the Holy Spirit and to be raptured. We must forsake the world and learn to commune with God at the altar of consecration. Such consecration and communion are imperative.

In Egypt there was generally no famine; yet even when it had had such, it only had its old grain for relief. In Canaan, however, there seemed to have been frequent famine. This, spiritually speaking, indicates to us that in the world there is little or no famine for the one who is not only in the world but of the world as well; but for the person who is in the way of obedience to God, there will sometimes *be* famine; for by comparison there is little or no trial in the world, whereas in the way of obedience there may be much trial. Nevertheless, this is the way to power and to rapture. Yet however great is the trial, with God there is always a living way out (see 1 Cor. 10.13). Hence let us be watchful as well as faithful. If we are not watchful we will fall back into Egypt, where there is neither consecration nor communion with God. To stay in Egypt, even temporarily, is to sin for a time. How pitiful should anyone ever take up his *permanent* residence there. Though he may avoid trial, in Egypt there is no altar.

Some people are like Abraham who did not go to Egypt all at once. He first moved towards the South, which was *in the direction* towards Egypt although he had not yet *arrived* in Egypt. To be in the South may be described spiritually as belonging half to the world and half to God. But in the South there is also no altar—no communion with God. Bethel, on the other hand, is an absolutely separated place. It is neither the Egypt of the world nor the South of worldly compromising.

It has been estimated that between two and three million Israelites came out of Egypt, yet God had not allowed a single one of them to have an altar in Egypt. For them to serve God at all, it was necessary for them to leave Egypt and to travel three days' journey beyond! (Ex. 8.25–27) In Egypt they might indeed have the passover because God had there delivered them from the penalty of sin which was death; but for them to come under the name of the Lord and to worship Him, they must *leave* Egypt.

3. Jericho (v.4)—Dealing with Satan

The clearest reference concerning the significance of Jericho is found in the book of Joshua. There we can observe the conquest of the entire city of Jericho.

"Joshua charged them with an oath at that time, saying, Cursed be the man before Jehovah, that riseth up and buildeth this city Jericho" (6.26). Thus Jericho means being cursed. This portion of Biblical history narrates how the children of Israel overcame their enemies for the first time in Canaan. The various peoples in Canaan, spiritually speaking, represent the evil spirits who belong to the devil. These can be likened to the spiritual hosts of wickedness in high places mentioned in Ephesians 6.12. And these are the enemies with which we believers fight today.

We need not only to overcome the flesh and the world, we must also overcome the enemy. There is only one way to overcome him: by believing in God's word and acting accordingly. We believe that we will obtain the promised result by acting according to His word. God has spoken, and this is enough. The people living in today's Jericho say they have the city, but we say we believe in God's word. They say their walls reach to heaven, but we say that our God is in heaven. They say all the territory included in the city is theirs, but we say God has promised to give us every place whereon the sole of our feet shall tread (see Joshua 1.3).

Many people know only the battle between the spirit and the flesh; they do not perceive the conflict that rages between us believers and the evil spirits as described in the sixth chapter of Ephesians. The real spiritual battle is fought between us and Satan with his evil spirits. This battle is joined by all matured believers, for the children of God on earth are frequently attacked by evil spirits. Such attacks sometimes occur in the believers' environment, sometimes in their physical bodies, sometimes in their thoughts, sometimes in their emotions, and sometimes in their spirits. Especially in this last hour the evil forces shall redouble their efforts to prevent believers from serving the Lord well by causing them to be distressed over many things. Too often believers are not aware of being attacked by evil spirits. They do not understand why everything seems to be against them, creating terrible confusion and trouble. They too often take these things as natural, not realizing that they are being supernaturally oppressed by the evil spirits.

In this last hour it is of utmost importance for believers to recognize their enemy and to know how to fight and overcome him. Even if we have overcome the flesh and the world, we will not be able to make great progress if we fail to overcome the works of the enemy. The fall of Jericho of old could not be attributed at all to human strength but to (1) the word of God and (2) the position the children of Israel took. To overcome the attack of the evil spirits, we (1) must not be mindful of circumstance and feeling but believe in the word of God's promise, thus putting the enemy to flight; and (2) must stand in the heavenly position which Christ has given to us, thereby keeping Satan and his evil spirits on the lower ground.

Without the word of God and without taking the position God has given us by faith, there can be no victory over the enemy.

4. The River Jordan (vv.6–14)—Dealing with Death

The river Jordan points to the power of death; and hence crossing the Jordan River is overcoming death. And that is rapture.

This facet of the journey has a special relationship to the Lord Jesus, since the Lord was himself baptized in the river Jordan. His having gone down into the waters of baptism signifies death. His coming up out of the water denotes resurrection. He overcomes death through the power of resurrection. The greatest power of Satan, we know, is death itself (see 1 Cor.

15.26). It is as if the Lord challenges His enemy by saying, Do whatever you can to Me (cf. Heb. 2.14). And Satan indeed does his uttermost. But God has the power of resurrection. Satan aspires to put the Lord to total death, yet the Lord has a life which cannot be touched or held by death. The Lord, as it were, goes through on dry ground! Apart from the Lord's resurrection, there is no power which can overcome death. The life which we receive at the time of regeneration is this very resurrection life. And the power of resurrection life will sweep away all death.

Crossing the Red Sea and crossing the Jordan River are quite different in significance. Crossing the Red Sea is an event that was forced by circumstance. The children of Israel were pursued by the enemy Egyptians; they would have been slaughtered had they not crossed it. Crossing the river Jordan, however, was a voluntary and self-chosen action. Some people today refuse to cross the river Jordan; they do not seek after the power of resurrection. But Paul highly esteemed that power, and so he pursued diligently after it (Phil. 3.10–12). All God's children have been resurrected with the Lord; nonetheless, many do not know experientially the power of the Lord's resurrection in their lives. Therefore these do not experience victory over death.

At this time in history when rapture is near, believers must finally overcome the last enemy—which is death. We must overcome death, whether physical or mental or spiritual. The world today is full of a deathly atmosphere. On the one hand, many used by the Lord often suffer physical weakness and illness. On the other hand, the minds of many saints seem to be paralyzed; their thinking, memory and concentration are not as alert as before. Furthermore, the spirits of many believers appear to be enveloped in death; their spirits are inactive, powerless, withered, paralyzed, and unable to cope with environment. Consequently, in these days of preparing for rapture, believers must learn to cross the Jordan River—as it were, to overcome death. We must learn to resist its power in our body as well as in our circumstances. We must prove the power of resurrection in all things. We must testify more and more to the fact that our Lord has been raised from the dead and that we who are joined to Him have also been raised.

In order to receive the outpoured Spirit of Elisha and to arrive at the rapture of Elijah, we must start out from Gilgal and travel forward till we reach and pass through the river Jordan. For the Holy Spirit can only descend upon those who are full of resurrection life. Do not imagine that so long as we are regenerated we will be raptured. God cannot rapture one who is not ready. Hence before there can take place a rapture like Elijah's we must go through the experiences of Gilgal, Bethel, Jericho, and the Jordan River.

God tells us that we will be raptured; so let us go the way we ought to go—commencing from Gilgal and ending on the other side of Jordan. And we shall find that God is there waiting for us!